Adieu Audrey

Memories of Audrey Hepburn

She was the physical embodiment of every teenager's dream, living evidence that fairy tales are real and that angels can come down to earth. This book is dedicated to Audrey Hepburn, who died in January 1993 — as a token of parting, in homage, and in memory of her.

She was born in Brussels in 1929. Her mother was a Dutch baroness, and her father was an Irish banker, who was soon to leave them. Her childhood, spent in English boarding schools and on the family's country estate in Arnhem, was over-shadowed by the war; however, this did not prevent her from working hard towards the career as a prima ballerina that she was hoping for. She studied at a famous London ballet school, made her living from temporary jobs, received her first engagements as a chorus girl in musicals and revues, and took cameo roles in a few British comedy films. Her big break came in 1951, when Colette, during the shooting of a film in Monte Carlo, discovered by chance a girl with expressive eyes who was rather too tall and too thin, and insisted that Audrey Hepburn, then a complete unknown, should take the lead part in the Broadway production of her play, *Gigi*. Hollywood pounced on her at once, and during the 1950s and 1960s her film triumphs followed — *Roman Holiday*, *Sabrina*, *Breakfast at Tiffany's*, *Charade*, and *My Fair Lady* — triumphs that were all the more astonishing since she did not really match the usual Hollywood clichés. Petite, almost androgynous, and with a disarming naturalness, she even had a worldwide impact on fashion and beauty trends for a time: her pillbox hats and tailored French suits, her short, tomboy hairstyle, and her flat shoes were copied by millions. Hollywood's sharpest tongue, Billy Wilder, complained she would soon even make breasts go out of fashion.

This book, with a text by Klaus-Jürgen Sembach, includes the best film stills, portraits, and private photographs by well-known and by unknown photographers from all over the world, who have provided us with an immortal image of Holly-wood's most endearing star.

136 pages, 76 duotone and 13 colour illustrations

Adieu Audrey

Memories of Audrey Hepburn

With a text by Klaus-Jürgen Sembach

Schirmer Art Books

Printed on Galerie Art Silk from M-real

Translation from the German by Michael Robertson

Schirmer Art Books is an imprint of
Schirmer / Mosel Verlag GmbH, Munich.
For trade information please contact:
Schirmer Art Books, John Rule, 40 Voltaire Rd.
London SW4 6DH, England or
Schirmer / Mosel Verlag, P.O. Box 401723, 80717 München, Germany
Fax 089 / 33 86 95

A CIP catalogue record for this book
is available from the British Library.

Lithos: O.R.T. Kirchner, Berlin
Typesetting: Typ-O-Graph, Munich
Printed by: EBS, Verona

ISBN 3-88814-566-X
A Schirmer / Mosel Production

Contents

Audrey Hepburn

One day, Bambi stepped out of the forest and took on human shape. This might be an American view of how Audrey Hepburn arrived on the scene, a view emphasizing her naïvety. But the way in which a charming artificial Bambi was transformed into a similar real person involved realms of the projection of human yearnings in which superficial, fairy-tale elements alone are no longer what count. What actually happened was that an ideal image reawoke that we had all thought vanished for ever. Add a touch of enchantment — and what happened next will be no surprise to those in the know: Undine stepped ashore, and the water-nymph became a woman.

*

Hollywood achieved many transformations, and Audrey Heburn's was not the first of its type. D. W. Griffith gave Lillian Gish, another waif-like figure, a similar breakthrough at the very beginning of film history. But she was lacking in energy on film, and she quickly faded away when talking pictures came in. Between Lillian Gish's return to stage acting in 1930 and Audrey Hepburn's appearance, there was an interval of almost three decades, in which quite different character types dominated. The German actress Elisabeth Bergner represented a similar type of figure, but she was mainly a stage actress, and the few films she made were little known outside continental Europe. She was only really a star around 1930, when her air of subtle refinement matched the times perfectly. But there is a direct link between the two actresses, as a quarter of a century later Audrey Hepburn featured in a remake of her *Ariane* — a part that was full of crafty innocence. It was not Hepburn's fault that the older film in the end remained the more subtle version; her choice of the film as a role model had been the correct one.

Other European influences also made themselves felt. She was moulded not only by her early years in Holland and England and by her multilingual education, but also by the subjects and settings of her first films — stories far removed from everyday life, un-American stories, preferably set in Paris, in Rome, Moscow, London, or in the isolated world of a Belgian convent. As early as *Roman Holiday*, which made her a star overnight, her character was marked out: a princess visiting Rome incognito, a story of bitter-sweet love left unfulfilled, but no real tragedy. A dream with the required minor calamity at the end, to preserve a veneer of credibility. At the time no one else could have performed the part but the fresh new actress, and the critics were caught unawares and with their guard down. Immediately

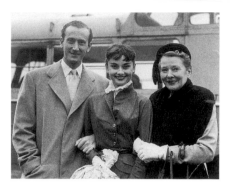

London, 30 September 1952: Audrey Hepburn about to fly to New York to play Gigi on Broadway, with her first fiancé James Hanson and her mother, Baroness van Heemstra.

afterwards, *Sabrina* reduced her to a Cinderella, but as we know, Cinderellas are only princesses in disguise. But this sort of person is now expected to be able to cook, something best learnt in Europe — or in Paris, to be precise; then you are sure to be turned into capital in America.

It was only later on that the fictional world in which Audrey Hepburn moved as a film star began to become more realistic. The transition from the 1950s to the 1960s brought to a close the phase in which she inhabited the artistically naïve world of illusion that Hollywood was supposed to typify. The moment had come in which *Sabrina* gave up *Love in the Afternoon*, relinquished her *Funny Face*, and instead appeared in a western and enjoyed a dubiously frugal *Breakfast at Tiffany's*. Now she had really made it in America.

But the people who had a formative influence on Audrey Hepburn were also European. It sounds like a classic fairy tale — better than the invented ones that were to follow — when we read that the most dignified representative of French libertinism, Madame Colette, insisted that Audrey Hepburn was the ideal embodiment of her Gigi. At the start of her career, Hepburn had so far only danced in a few sketches and taken small parts in British films, and it was Colette who opened up America for her. Her breakthrough on Broadway made the rest easy. In one of the intervals between her first Hollywood films she returned to the stage once more as Undine — as the figure she herself in a sense really was.

In spite of his American name, William Wyler, her first great director, actually came from Mulhouse in Alsace, which was part of Germany when he was born. After studying in Lausanne and Paris, he went to the United States when he was twenty, encouraged to emigrate by Carl Laemmle, a distant relation, who was a legendary early tycoon and founder of Universal Pictures, a studio with a preference for horror films. In Hollywood, Wyler created tragedies such as *Jezebel*, *Wuthering Heights*, *Mrs. Miniver*, and *The Best Years of Our Lives*, in which stars such as Bette Davis, Greer Garson, and Laurence Olivier appeared. *Roman Holiday*, with the young Audrey Hepburn, was for Wyler an unusual and late departure into a lighter genre.

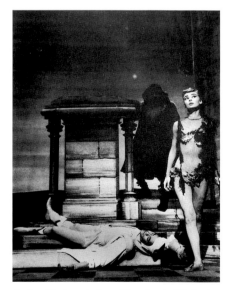

Audrey Hepburn in Jean Giraudoux's 'Undine' with Mel Ferrer, 1954.

Luckily, the film succeeded in being sentimental without reducing itself to kitsch. The story line concealed countless possible traps, but miraculously they were all avoided. A lucky star was obviously watching over this 'affair of the heart', which could hardly fail to be a resounding success with the public. *Roman Holiday* was one of the most memorable films of the 1950s. It certainly reproduced one of the period's most secret ideals, that of spotless innocence, together with a hint of unreality. Audrey Hepburn played with astonishing assurance for a beginner, and a great deal of her own personality went into the part — as everyone could see.

There was special importance, too, in the fact that Paramount, in order to use up some frozen resources, had decided to produce the film in Italy itself, and with an usually high proportion of outdoor shots. This meant not only that the backgrounds were more authentic than usual, but also that the new star's physical appearance remained undistorted. Two more films with William Wyler followed over the next two years: *The Children's Hour* and *How to Steal a Million*.

Even more so than Wyler, Austrian-born Billy Wilder combined a European training — particularly his experience in Berlin — with American know-how. His cynicism, which was sometimes rather too bitter for American tastes, was complemented by a relentless gift for observation. *Sabrina* and *Love in the Afternoon* were certainly not intended to be watched entirely without discomfort. In the years before and after these films, Wilder worked with stars such as Gloria Swanson, Kirk Douglas, and Marilyn Monroe in *Sunset Boulevard*, *Ace in the Hole*, and *Some Like it Hot*, films in which the tone was somewhat rougher. Large parts of *Sabrina*, too, were rather callous in their effect, and the overemphatic presentation of Hepburn in it meant that she had already lost something of her incomparable quality. Hollywood standards had imposed themselves.

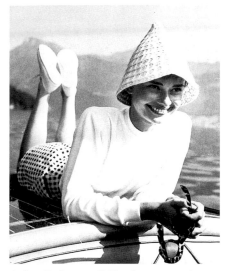

Audrey Hepburn in 1954 in her private refuge in Switzerland.

It may not have been Wilder's explicit intention, although it showed his typical sensitivity, that he cast Audrey Hepburn alongside partners who were obviously older than her. It began with Humphrey Bogart — casting him in a romantic part was already cynical enough — and continued with Fred Astaire, Gary Cooper, Cary Grant, and Rex Harrison. In *War and Peace*, too, Audrey Hepburn in the end chooses Henry Fonda, the oldest of the men around her. All of her co-stars were distinguished father-figures providing a sophisticated backdrop against which her innocence and fragility could be displayed. Younger actors were easily overshadowed by Audrey Hepburn — even her own husband, Mel Ferrer, who wisely only appeared alongside her twice. Who now remembers William Holden, Anthony Perkins, or George Peppard playing opposite her? Immature, clumsy youths. It was only when Audrey Hepburn was older — and at the same time, with a more contemporary role image, seemed younger — that the vivacious Albert Finney was capable of being a real opposite number for her. Finally, Sean Connery was superb alongside her at a time when both of them were more mature.

Fred Zinnemann, like Wilder, had his origins in Austria, and the two had briefly met in Berlin earlier on. Zinnemann had been in the USA since 1929, but his career was slow to develop; it was only after the Second World War that he took the public by surprise with *High Noon* and *From Here to Eternity*, two extraordinarily powerful films that he followed up a few years later with a comparable work, *The Nun's Story*. This was perhaps the most serious film that Audrey Hepburn made, and its seriousness was due not only to the stature of its principal star, but also to the credibility and dignity she brought to the role of a novice plagued by doubts and contradictions. Her interpretation of the role was supported by the film's almost documentary approach — and the scenes set in Africa are remarkable anticipations of Audrey Hepburn's later activities there. Apart from being a surprisingly big commercial success, the film brought Audrey Hepburn an Oscar nomination as principal actress — she had already had one for *Sabrina* and would later also

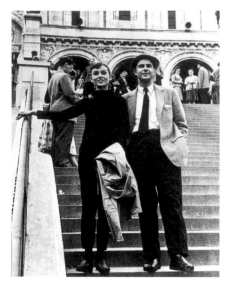

With director Stanley Donen in Paris, 1956.

be nominated for *Breakfast at Tiffany's* and *Wait Until Dark*. Marked out for success from the very beginning of her career, she had already been awarded an Oscar for *Roman Holiday*.

In addition to European directors, a European cameraman was decisive for her as well — the Austrian Franz Planer, who worked on five of her films. Apart from John Huston's classic western *The Unforgiven*, the more subtle of her films were *Roman Holiday, The Nun's Story, Breakfast at Tiffany's*, and *The Children's Hour*, and the first two of these moulded her image more than any of the others. Planer was born in Karlovy Vary, now in the Czech Republic but then part of the Austrian Empire, and had worked in Berlin and Vienna. He had photographed the German film classic *Die Drei von der Tankstelle* (The Three from the Gas Station) as well as two of the most sensitive films of the early 1930s: Willi Forst's *Maskerade*, which owed its very precise structure to Planer, and Max Ophüls's *Liebelei*, which already had the luminous glow that Planer was later to give to Ophüls's *Letter from an Unknown Woman*. The latter was one of the few films Ophüls made in Hollywood, and Joan Fontaine was surely photographed in it more subtly than she had ever been before. As her successor in Planer's viewfinder, Audrey Hepburn benefited immensely from his familiarity with the culture of photography.

*

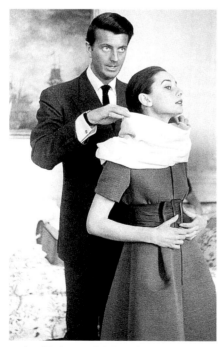

Audrey Hepburn and fashion designer Hubert de Givenchy. Their many years of collaboration began in 1953 on the costumes for 'Sabrina'.

It had never really been necessary for Hollywood to use costume designers from abroad, since the studios' own ones were far too good themselves — and their influence on what was being worn was greater than that of the Paris couturiers, who were capable of setting the tone, but only very indirectly. But now and then exceptions were made for the big names. Around 1930, Gloria Swanson was allowed to wear costumes by Coco Chanel, while after the war Marlene Dietrich chose her wardrobe at Dior's, and Audrey Hepburn was for many years a customer of Hubert de Givenchy. Givenchy's fresh, elegant suits, coats, and hats had exactly the same kind of spirit that made a film like *Charade* stand out. It was a film in which every element involved matched exactly: the story, the actors in the leading roles, the décor and costumes, and the director — not to mention the inventively designed title sequence and the music. In the meantime, Audrey Hepburn had escaped from being typecast as a young, timid girl, and she now advanced to the status of a young widow with a large inheritance. *Charade* was a perfect example of a comedy of manners that had a precise mixture of the ingredients tension, irony, and style. It was a brilliant innovation, and there were many attempts to imitate it. *How to Steal a Million* was one of these, again involving Hubert de Givenchy, but it was not so successful. What made the difference between the two films is obvious when Cary Grant is compared to Peter O'Toole as her opposite number. The older partner was an incomparably better match for her.

It was thirteen years after she made her début with him that William Wyler once again directed her in *How to Steal a Million*. In *Charade*, the director was an

American, Stanley Donen, a former dancer who later went on to become a choreographer, who had worked extensively with Gene Kelly. He also directed *Funny Face*, Audrey Hepburn's fourth Hollywood film, in which she had to prove herself as a singer and dancer alongside Fred Astaire. The film succeeded because, although the script called for Astaire to be her lover and in several scenes her dancing partner, his real co-star was the fabulous Kay Thompson (a marginal phenomenon on the horizon of American film, whose talent only Hollywood could have afforded to waste). Thompson was closer to Astaire in age as well, and was able to skilfully divert attention from any too detailed comparison between Astaire and Hepburn. An original, only lightly accompanied solo number in an existentialist dive in Paris gave Audrey Hepburn — who had to transform herself from being a shy New York bookstore assistant into a fantastically beautiful model — an opportunity to show her independence as a dancer. Numerous gowns by Hubert de Givenchy accompanied the furious train of events. In a later film, however, neither the Paris costumes nor the much-used locations could drive away the boredom — *Paris When It Sizzles* was an affected comedy that was hectic but lacked movement. A brief appearance by Marlene Dietrich very close to the beginning of the film made the rest of it forgettable, illuminating for a moment everything that was missing in it. Her older colleague knew exactly what was needed: she was seen — and this was the only reason for her appearance — on her way to Dior.

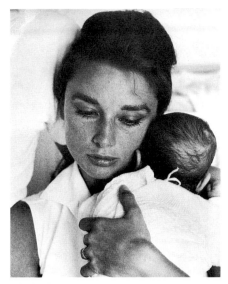

The birth of Audrey Hepburn's and Mel Ferrer's son Sean in 1960. Photo by Richard Avedon.

While Hubert de Givenchy's wardrobes always remained elements that fitted precisely into a larger whole, Cecil Beaton's exalted costumes — which were as vital to *My Fair Lady* as the sets, the music, and Rex Harrison as Professor Higgins were — ranked as 'stars' themselves. They even had a tendency to upstage the actress wearing them, and reinforced the impression that Eliza Doolittle was not the most suitable part for Audrey Hepburn. Her casting probably resulted from a calculation that a "safe" star was needed and that, with her intelligence, it was worth taking the risk that the role might fall apart. George Bernard Shaws's social satire *Pygmalion*, which, sweetened with music, is noticeably based on the worst possible operetta, is actually unperformable. Either Eliza Doolittle is genuine, in which case she can only turn herself at best into a kind of lesser Christiane Vulpius (Goethe's wife, who was also of lower social standing) through her rescuer's efforts to reform her, entering her new life merely with resignation; or from the very first she must be incapable of concealing the fact that she is actually a lady whose true identity has been obscured by a few silly accidents. But that cannot really be the point of the thing. Audrey Hepburn played the second of these two possibilities — what else — and her performance was therefore only half-satisfactory. If *My Fair Lady* succeeded in spite of this, it was due to the way in which the various ingredients were successfully mixed. These were mainly 'very British': Shaw, Beaton, Harrison, and — being generous — the former London drama student Hepburn. The American George Cukor, who as always was unobtrusively reliable as a dir-

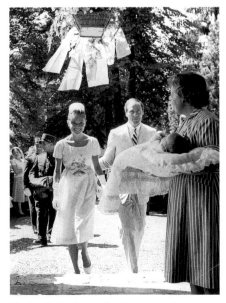

The family at the baptismal ceremony in Switzerland. Photo by Richard Avedon.

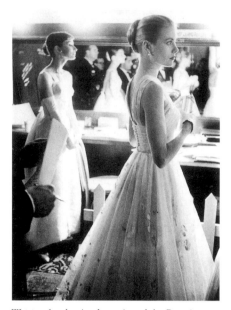

Waiting for the Academy Award for Best Actress, 1955. Audrey Hepburn receives the award for 'Sabrina', and Grace Kelly for 'The Country Girl'.

ector, had a 'continental' label on him anyway. The American film industry's strategy of always using only the most tried and tested participants once again proved itself, even if Audrey Hepburn only remained a figure playing a part.

*

'My Fair Lady' in real life: a physically awkward, but very ambitious singer wanted to look like Audrey Hepburn. She succeeded, and the world should therefore thank Audrey Hepburn for Maria Callas becoming the one and only Maria Callas. An ambitious film actress, unsuited to tragic parts but attached to the naïve genre, apparently wanted to look like Maria Callas, at least for a moment, which is why there are some photographs in which Audrey Hepburn looks like the great operatic heroine. More was not possible. But we are constantly moving at the highest possible artistic level here. Where are her female contemporaries? We hardly ever see them in Audrey Hepburn's company — although she and Grace Kelly meet on one occasion in the powder room of a ladies' toilet. It was an image that worked, as one could divine the future princess in Kelly. There was also a 'Garbo' aspect to Audrey Hepburn, above all her desire only to be present when working on location. Otherwise her address was Bürgenstock in Switzerland.

Her appearance in *My Fair Lady* had the involuntary, but unmistakable effect of making it clear that she was a modern woman, in spite of her complete lack of everyday qualities. The costume roles did not suit her, and remained merely a disguise. Certainly her character was only made possible by the way in which a certain toughness and firmness remained noticeable behind her superficial sweetness. From the very start, she was a charming personality, but with a will of her own. And it was obvious that in the course of time this would increasingly come to the fore. Her two last films, for the time being, cleverly underlined this. In *Two for the Road*, Audrey Hepburn was simply a young woman trying to save her marriage. Stanley Donen directed — the third time they had worked together — and he was obviously well aware of what suited her best. *Wait Until Dark* was a thriller on an intimate scale, in which innocence not only suffered, but for the first time was persistently persecuted. This was an effective way of expanding her range, and the film was highly successful. But she stopped acting after it, perhaps because she knew that further improvement as no longer possible. After such a successful career, which had been largely free of any vicissitudes, it was a smart move to get out while she was still at the top. But it was obvious at once that, in spite of her attempts to adapt, she was aging: the new, heavy eyeshadow ruined her face, as did modern beehive hair styles. She looked mistreated. She only returned to the screen nine years later in *Robin and Marian*, a touching film, but one that failed to meet with any wider resonance. Occasional appearances in films followed, none of which were really necessary. Audrey Hepburn died of cancer in 1993, at the age of sixty-three.

Towards the end, her attention had turned to other fields. Life in Paris, Switzerland, and — following her second marriage — in Rome had not been abandoned, and the 'star' still made appearances, but all of this was paralleled by her activity as a special emissary for UNICEF, the United Nations Children's Fund. She travelled to Africa and Latin America in many occasions, and the constantly varying situations she found herself in show that she was not just playing for effect. A woman whose place among the stars was already assured no longer needed to create effects. Her involvement was genuine, and it obviously gave her a real sense of fulfilment.

Was this surprising? In a peculiar fusion of fact and fiction, some of the parts she had played had already anticipated this development. Not only the title figure in *The Nun's Story*, but also Natasha in *War and Peace* transformed themselves from selfish girls into angels of mercy, at least for a time. *War and Peace* was one of her weakest films, and although the film's success apparently justified it, it ist almost unbearable to watch while she is being turned into a cliché. Her appearance in *War and Peace* made Audrey Hepburn extremely popular as a consolingly ethereal counterpart to the more sensual figures played by other actresses of the time — it is strange to think of her as the contemporary of Monroe and Bardot. But destiny's greatest gifts can be its most fateful ones, and Audrey Hepburn was surely aware of this danger from early on. Her whole subsequent life, as well as the film parts she played, can be seen as a steadfast effort to achive a deeper humanity. And we were privileged to watch as Audrey Hepburn movingly succeeded in this.

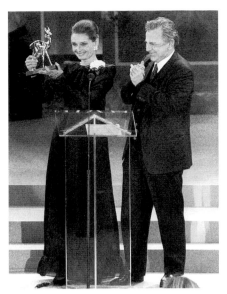

Wiesbaden, Germany, 1991: Maximilian Schell presents Audrey Hepburn with a Bambi award for her work as a special emissary for UNICEF.

Edda Kathleen van Heemstra Hepburn-Ruston is fourteen years old and firmly committed to becoming a prima ballerina. She takes ballet lessons at the Conservatory in her home town in Holland, Arnhem. The photo shows her in one of her first appearances on stage, ca. 1943.

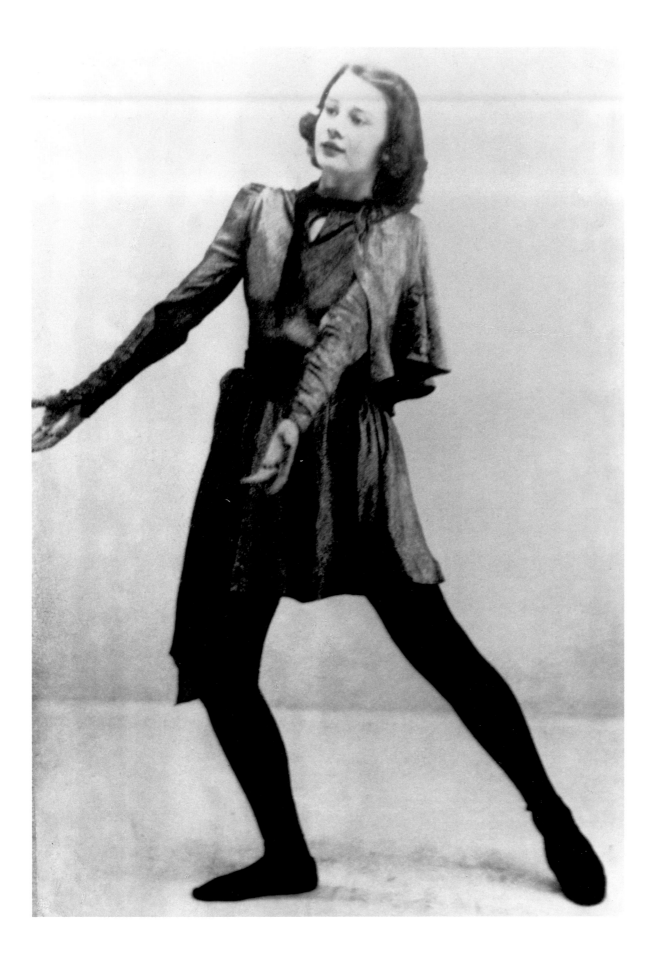

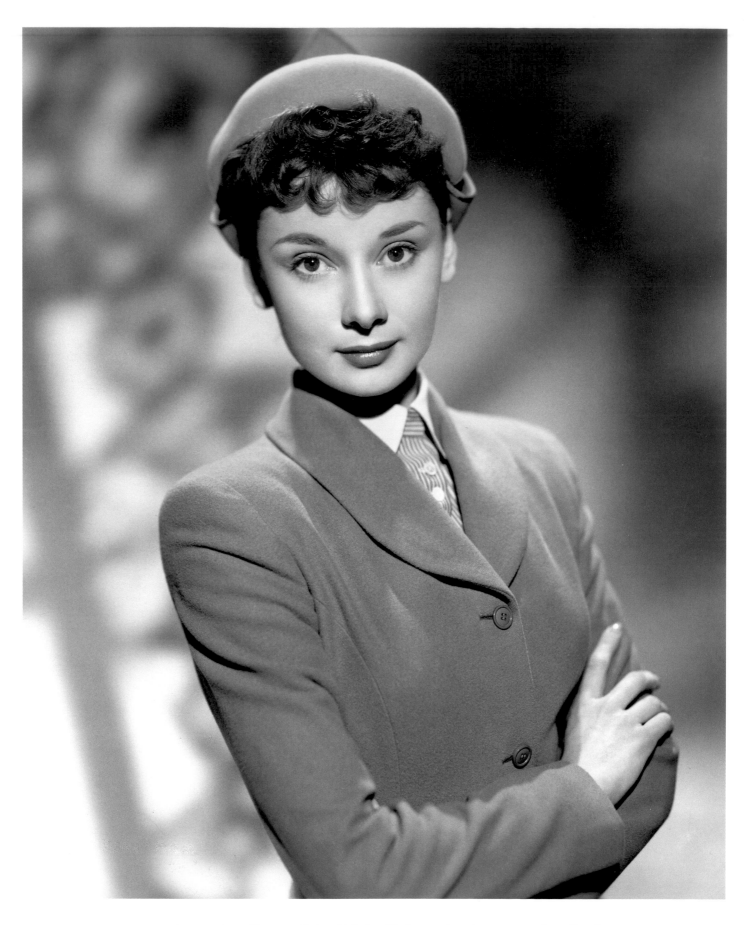

Stop-off in London. Edda now calls herself Audrey Hepburn and is playing minor roles in British comedy films. A publicity still for 'Young Wives' Tales', 1951.

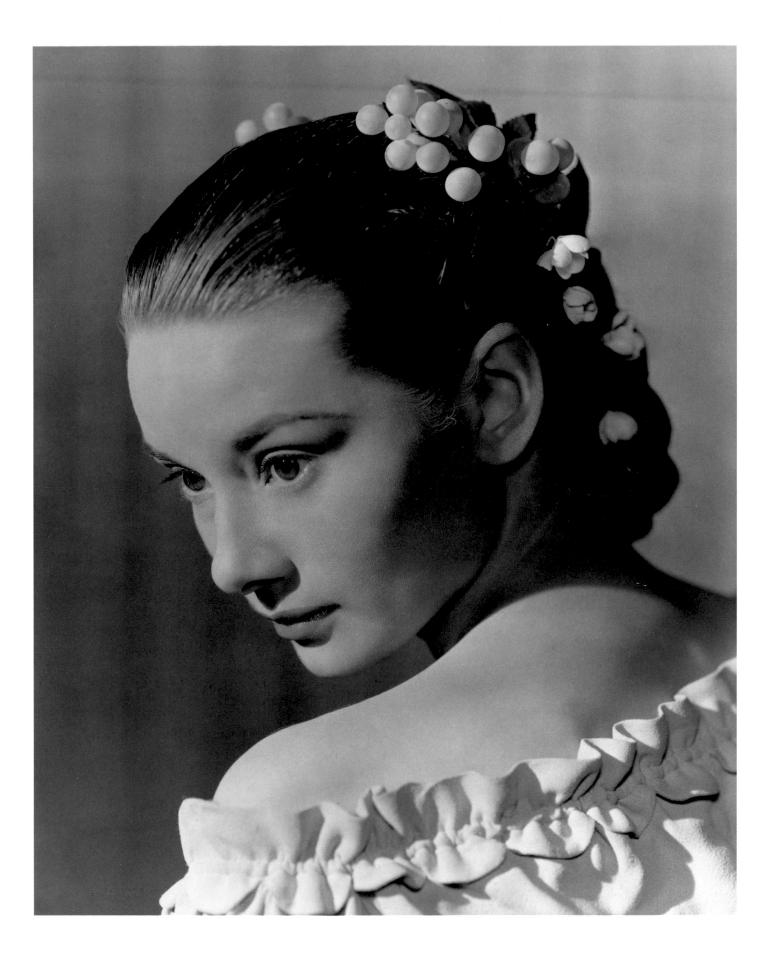

Publicity still, ca. 1950 / 51.

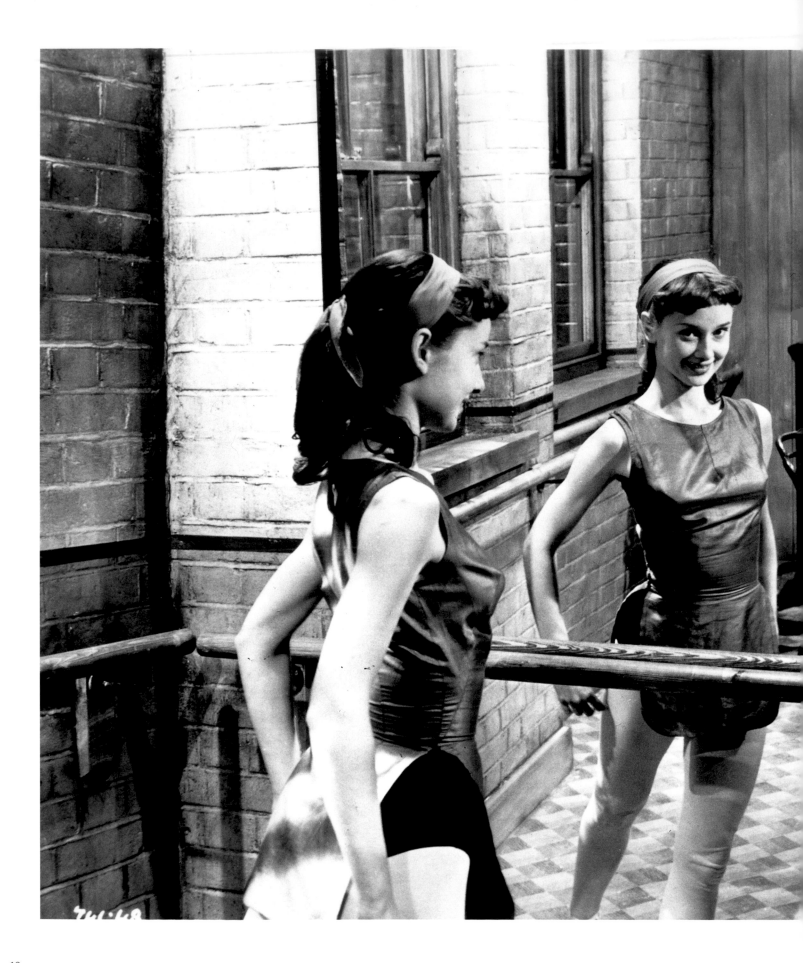

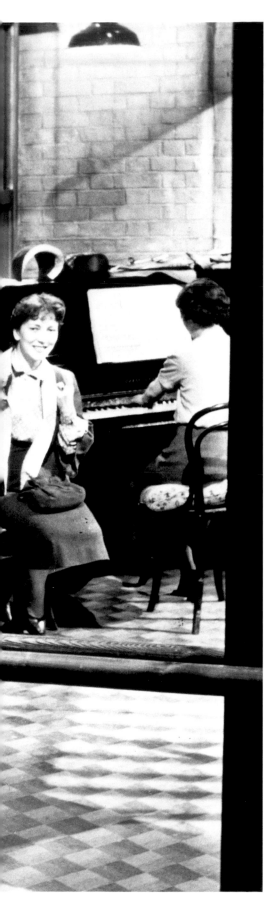

In the British spy thriller 'The Secret People', which came out in 1952, Audrey Hepburn faces the camera as a ballet student, who together with her sister in the story — Valentina Cortese, in the background — is looking for her father, who has disappeared.

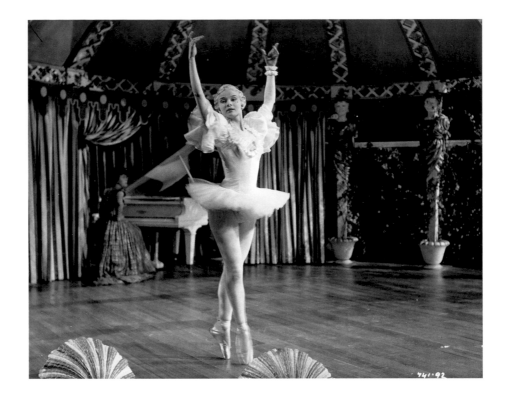

Above and right:
The fulfilment on the silver screen of her childhood dream: Audrey Hepburn as a ballerina with a
powdered wig and tutu in 'The Secret People'.

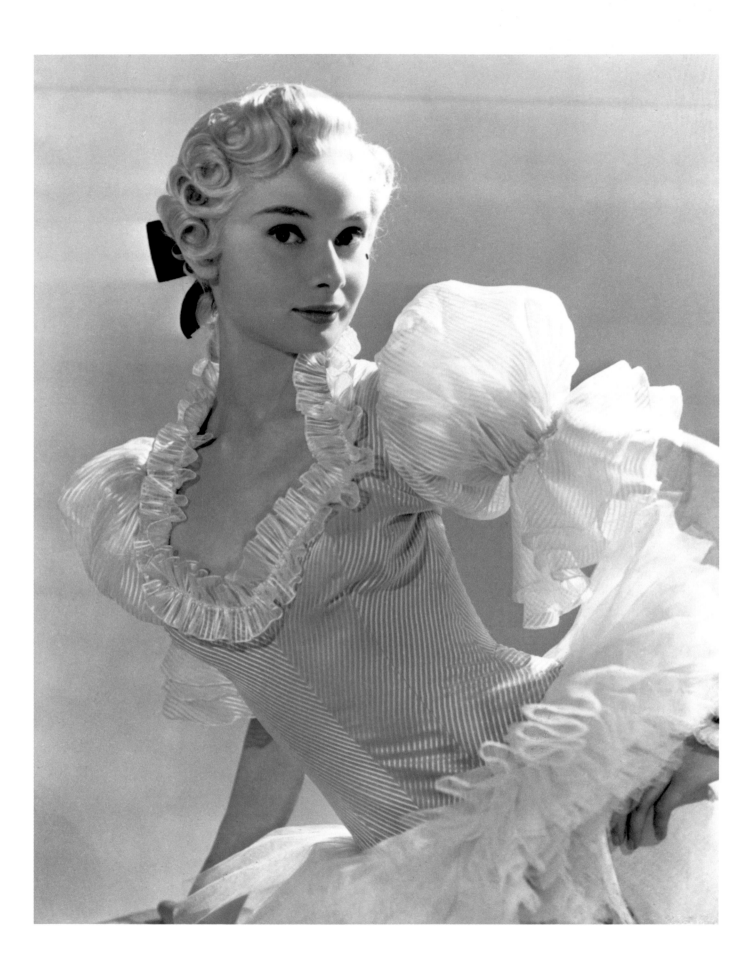

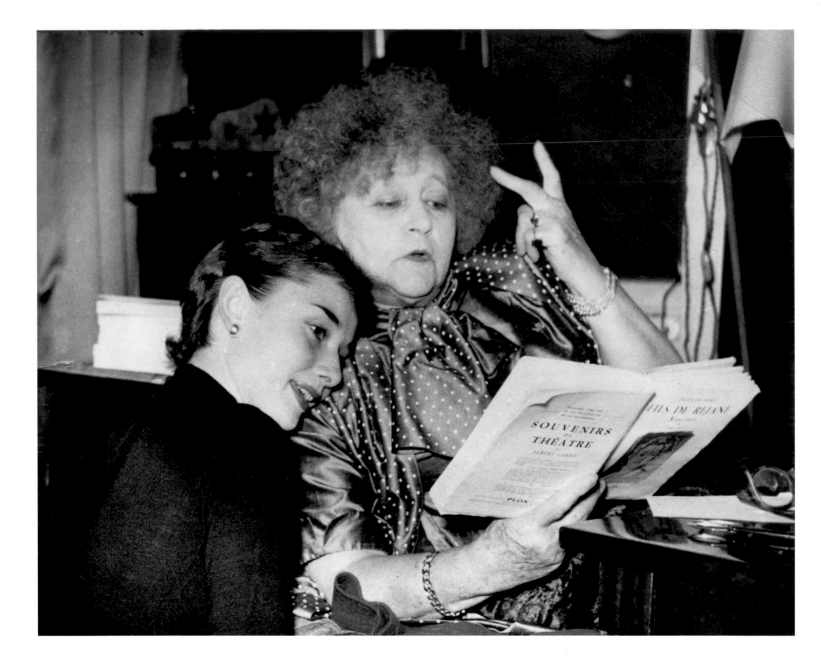

The big break. Colette, the 'grande dame' of French literature, discovers Audrey Hepburn by chance during the shooting of a film in Monte Carlo, and insists that Audrey Hepburn, then a complete unknown, should take the lead part in the Broadway stage version of her novel, 'Gigi'. Above: with Colette in Paris, 1951.

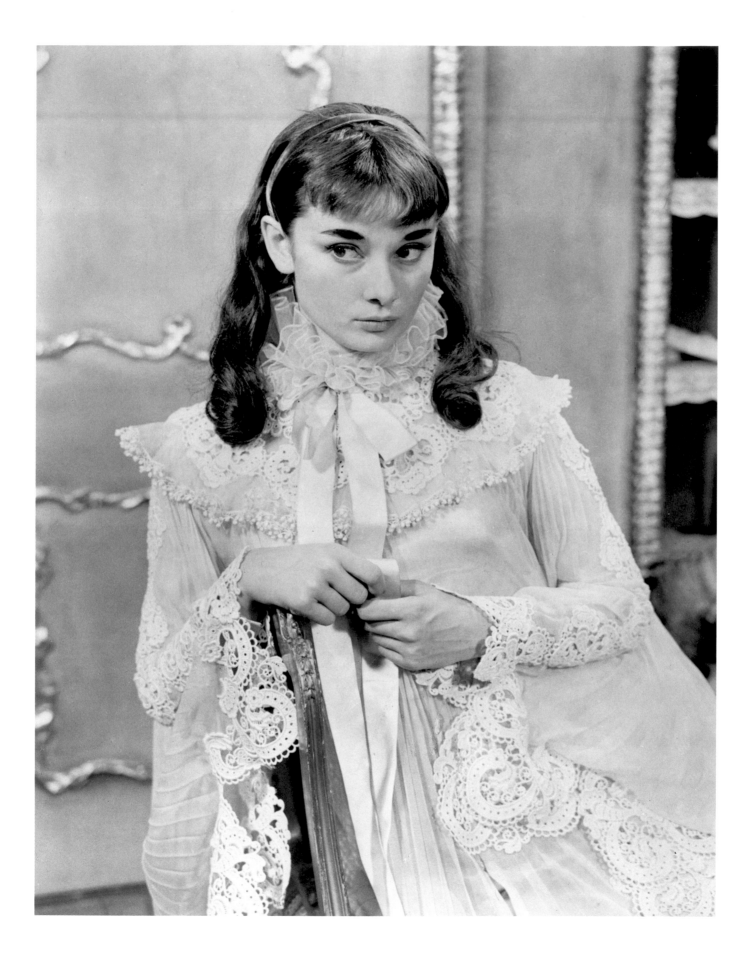

As Gigi on Broadway. 23

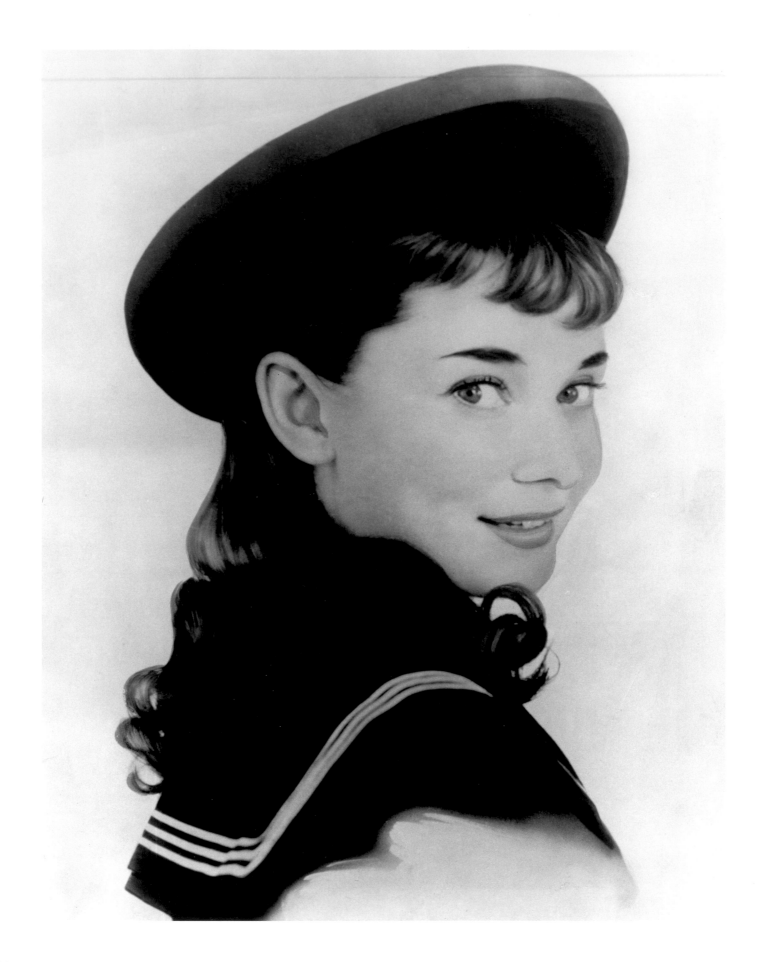

As Gigi, 1951.

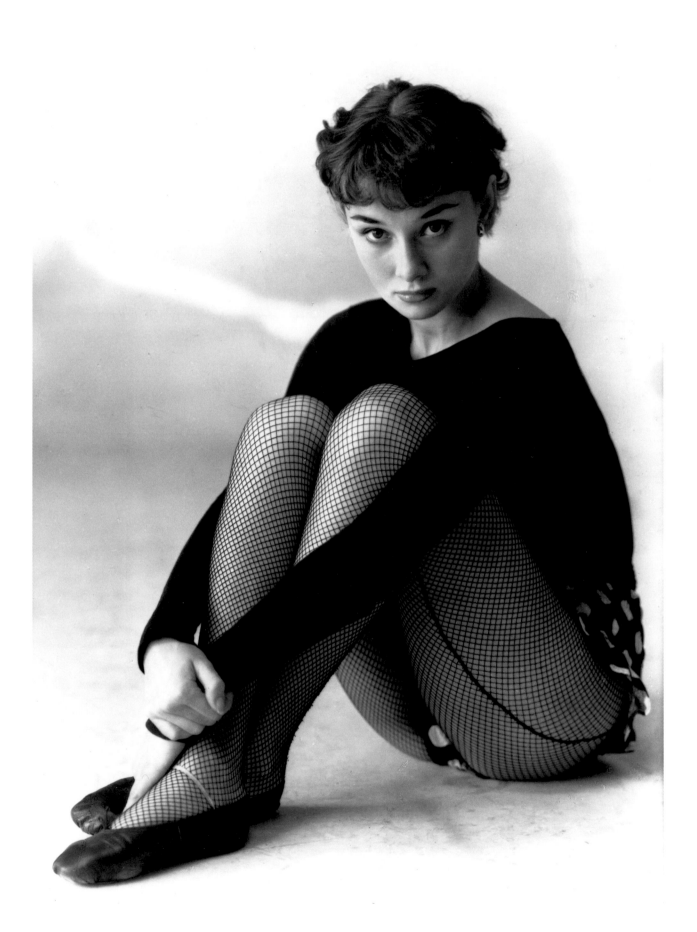

Portrait as a ballerina, ca. 1950. Photo: Bassano.

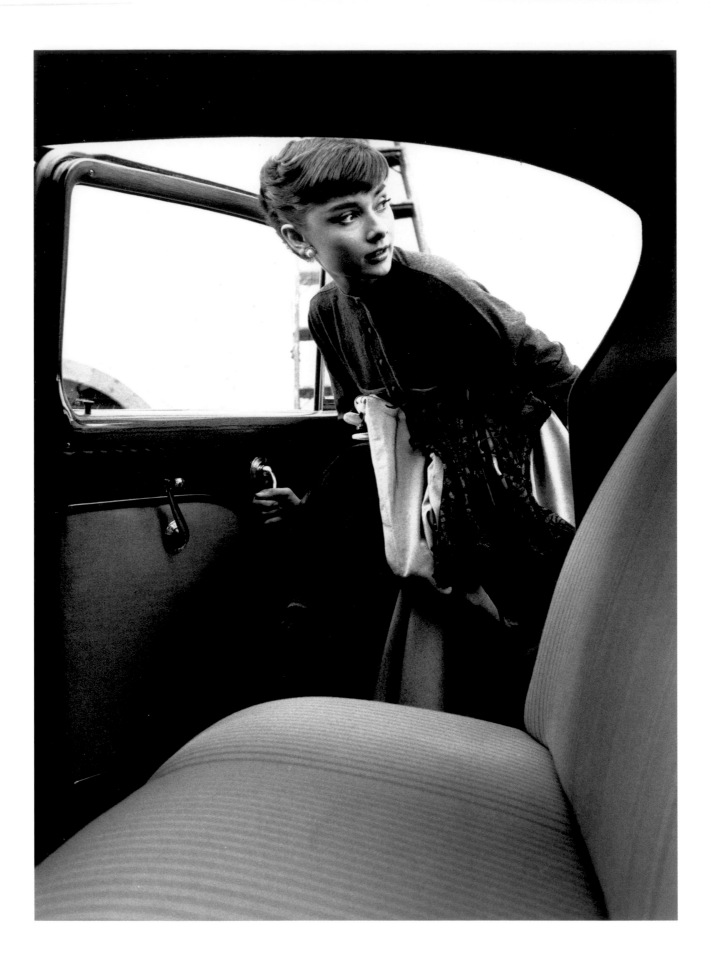

During her first visit to Paramont in Hollywood. Photo by Bob Willoughby.

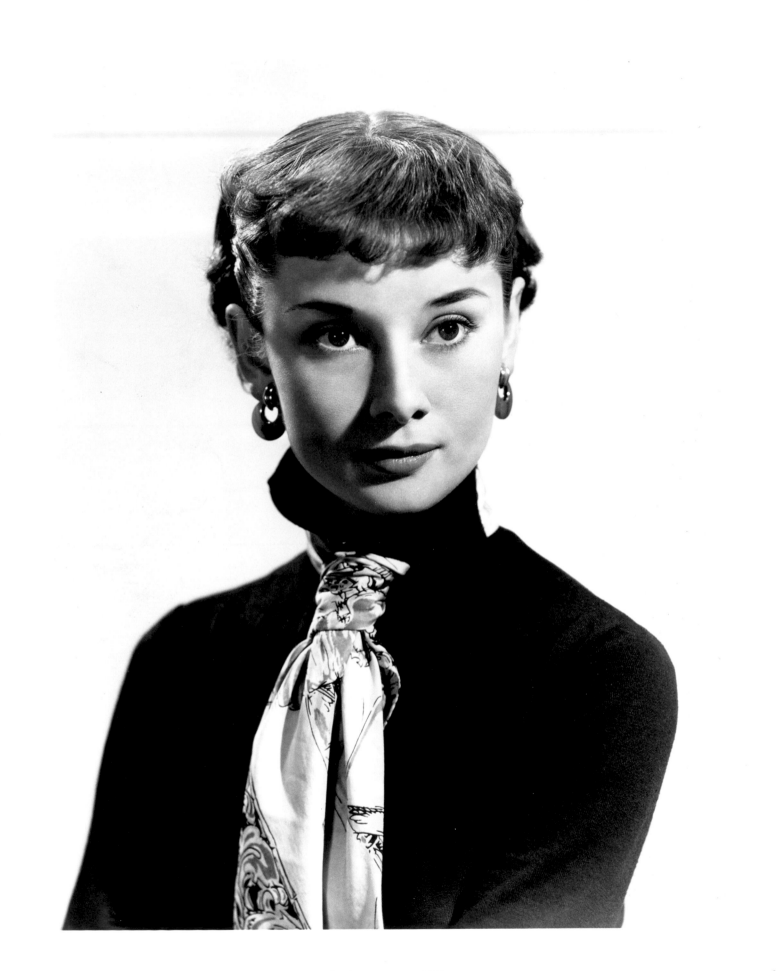

Studio portrait, ca. 1952.

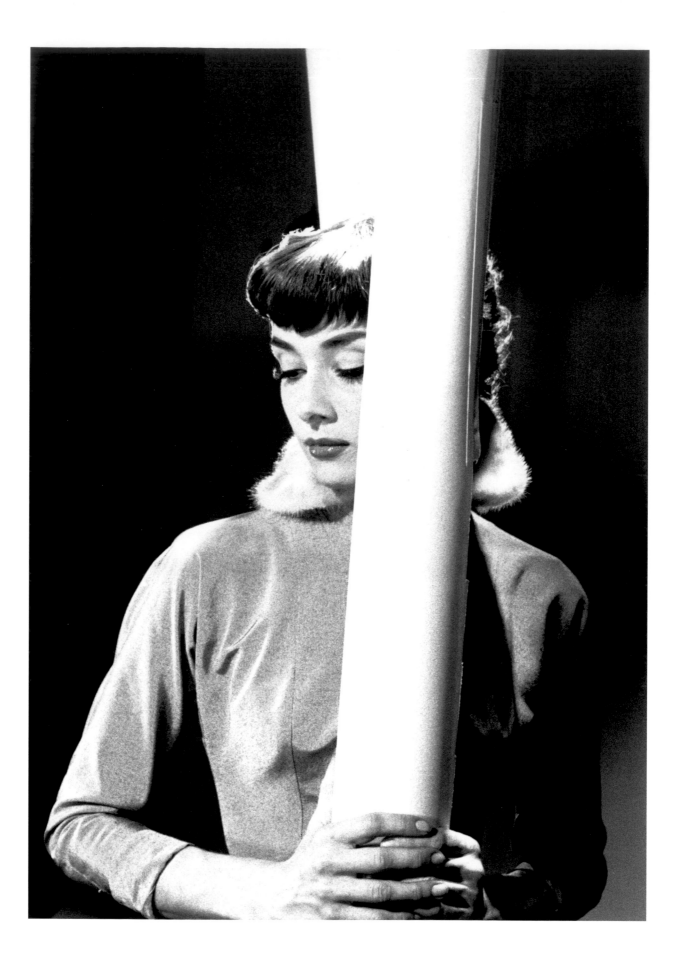

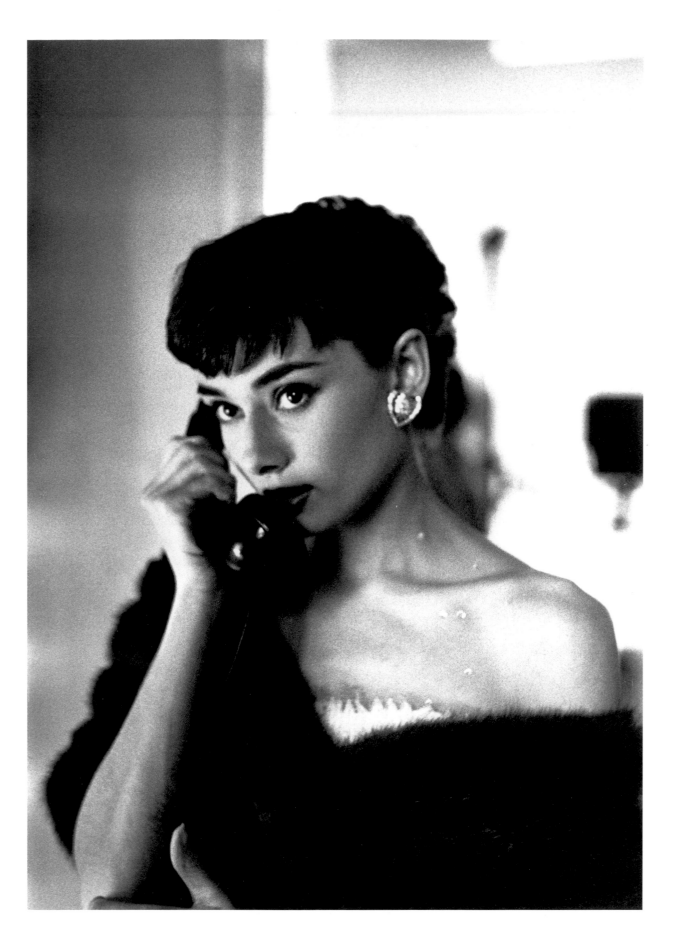

Above and left: Hollywood courting the new star.
Shots by Bob Willoughby from her camera test at Paramount Studios, 1953.

Colour portrait, ca. 1953.

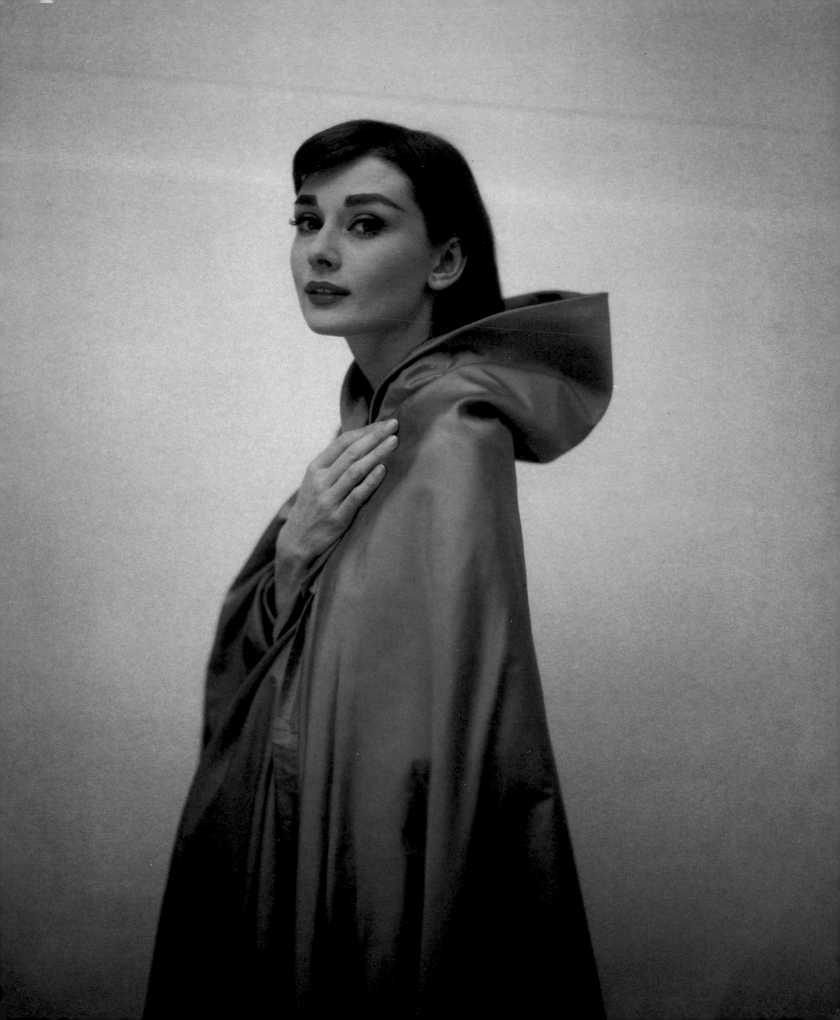

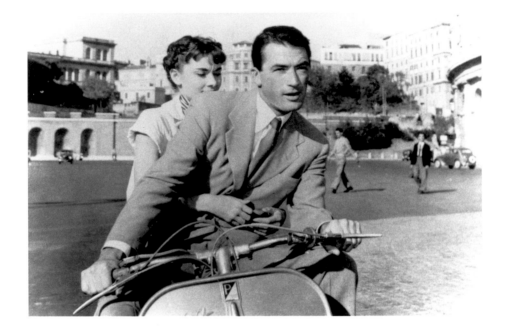

A princess incognito on a Vespa in Rome.
Audrey Hepburn and Gregory Peck in 'Roman Holiday', 1952.

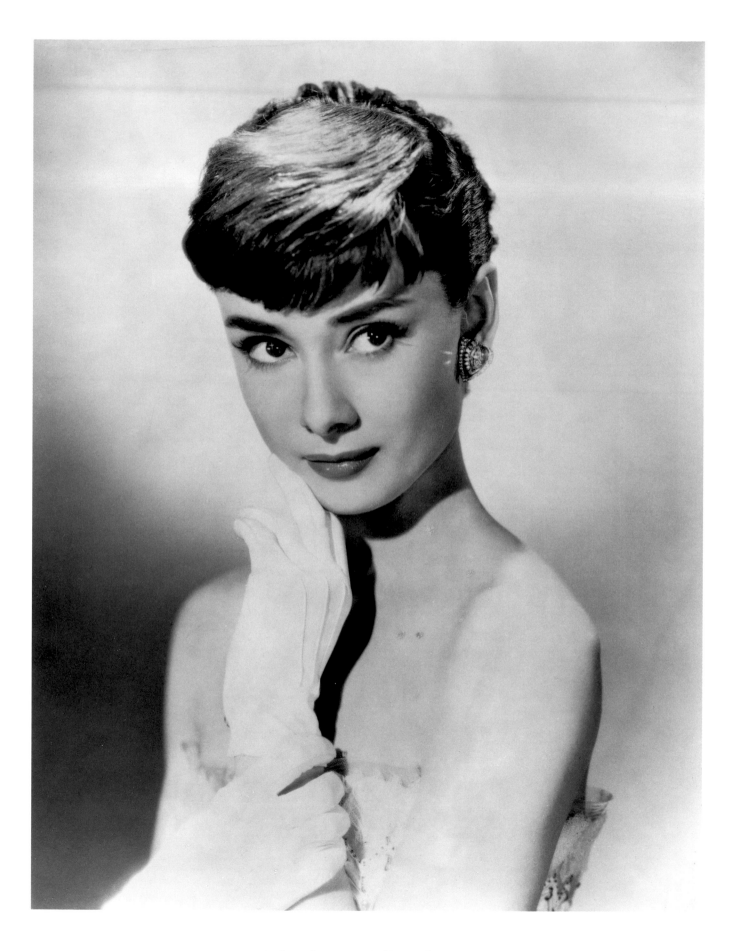

Hollywood's new star. Publicity still, ca. 1952.   33

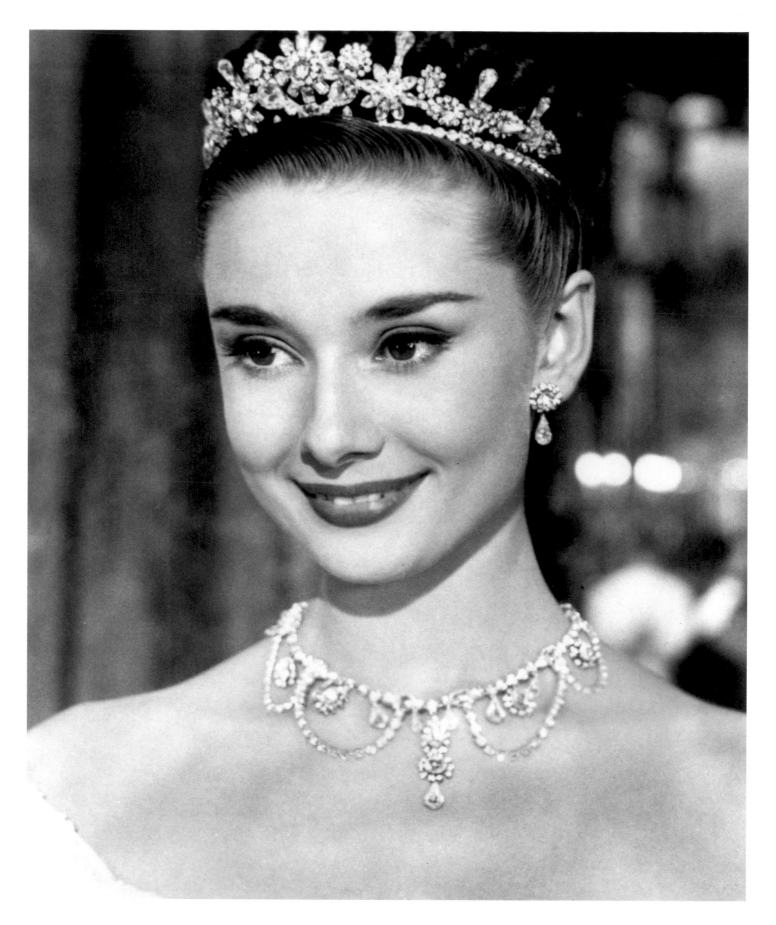

Audrey Hepburn as Princess Anne, dressed up to the nines.
Still from 'Roman Holiday', 1952.

35

'Sabrina', Audrey Hepburn's second Hollywood film and second worldwide hit, was made in New York, as well as other locations. Dennis Stock photographed her during shooting, 1953.

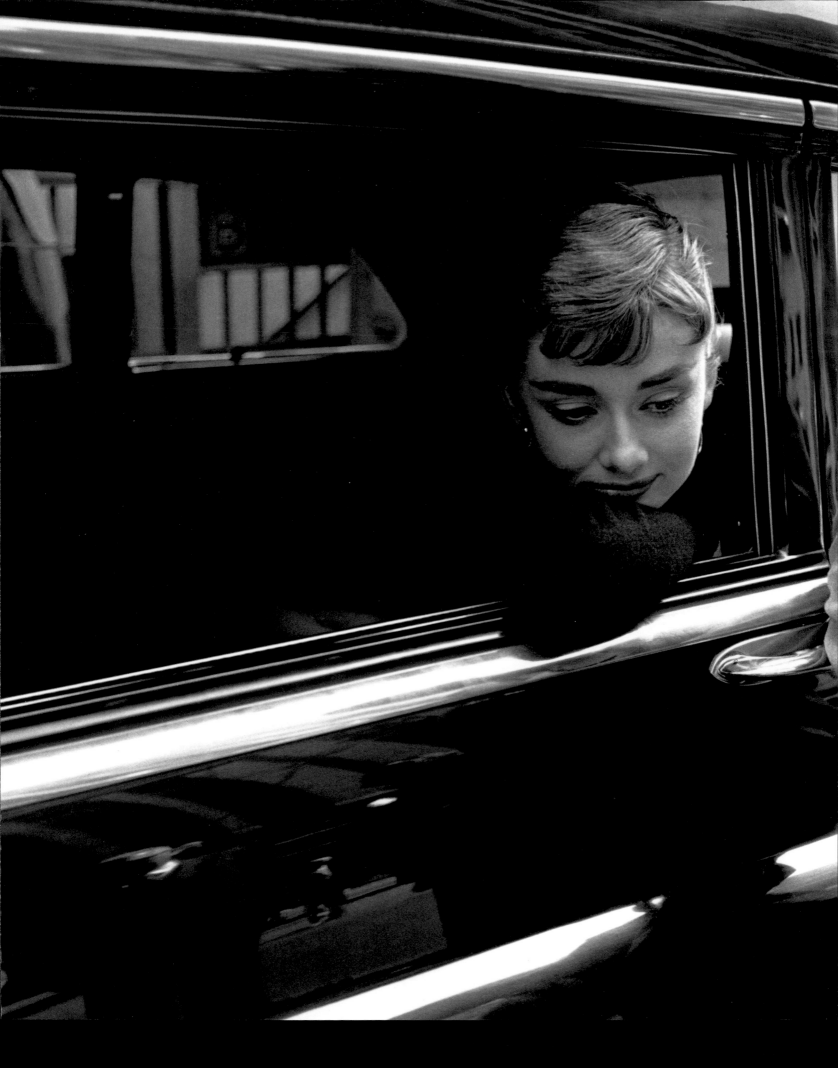

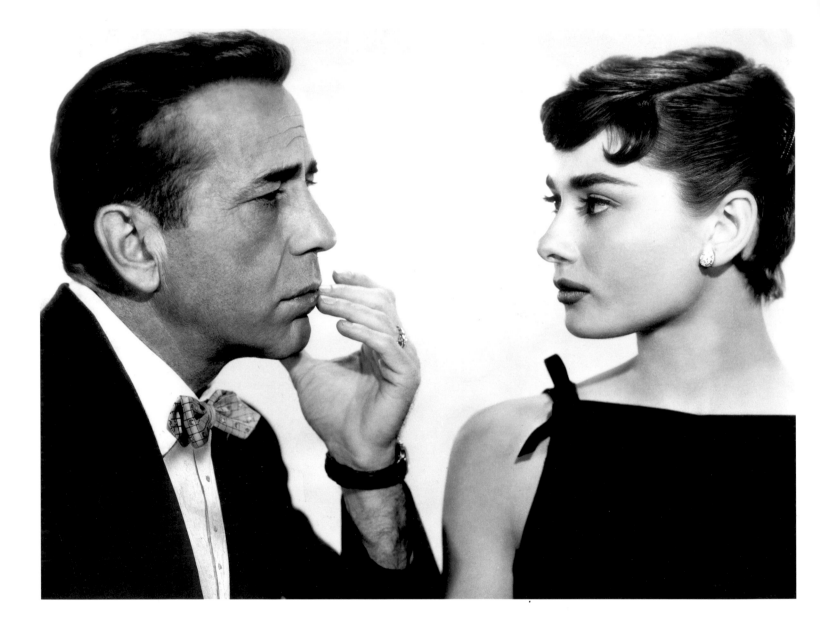

Audrey Hepburn as Sabrina. Her co-star, Humphrey Bogart, suddenly sees with new eyes the Cinderella who has been transfigured by Givenchy. 1953.

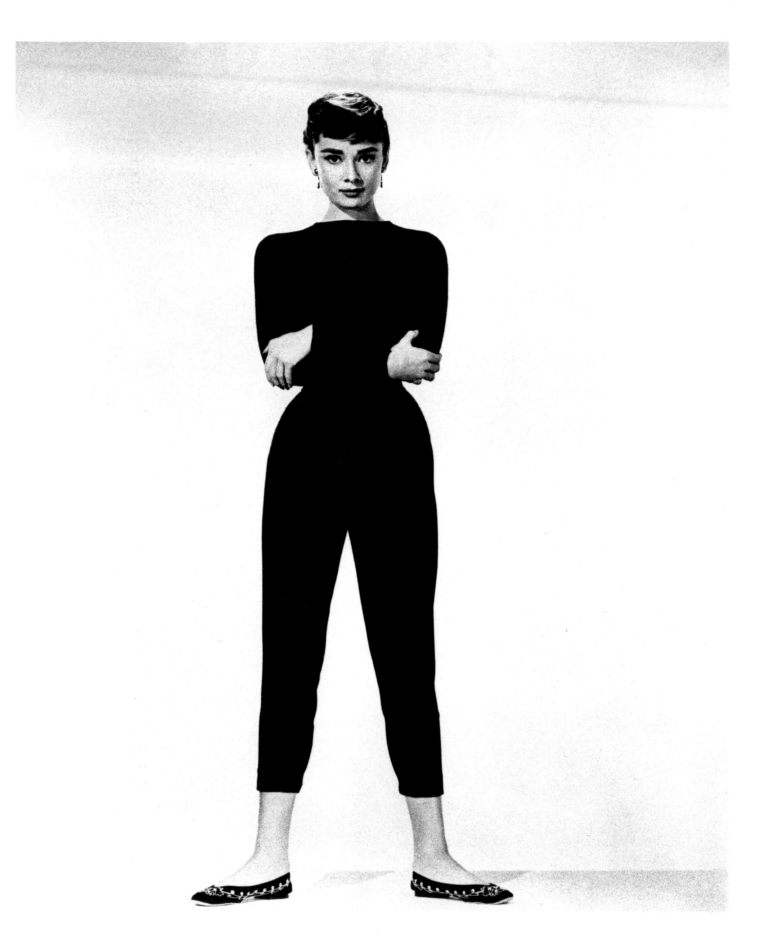

Above and following two pages: Publicity stills by Bud Fraker, Paramount's portrait photographer, for 'Sabrina', 1954.

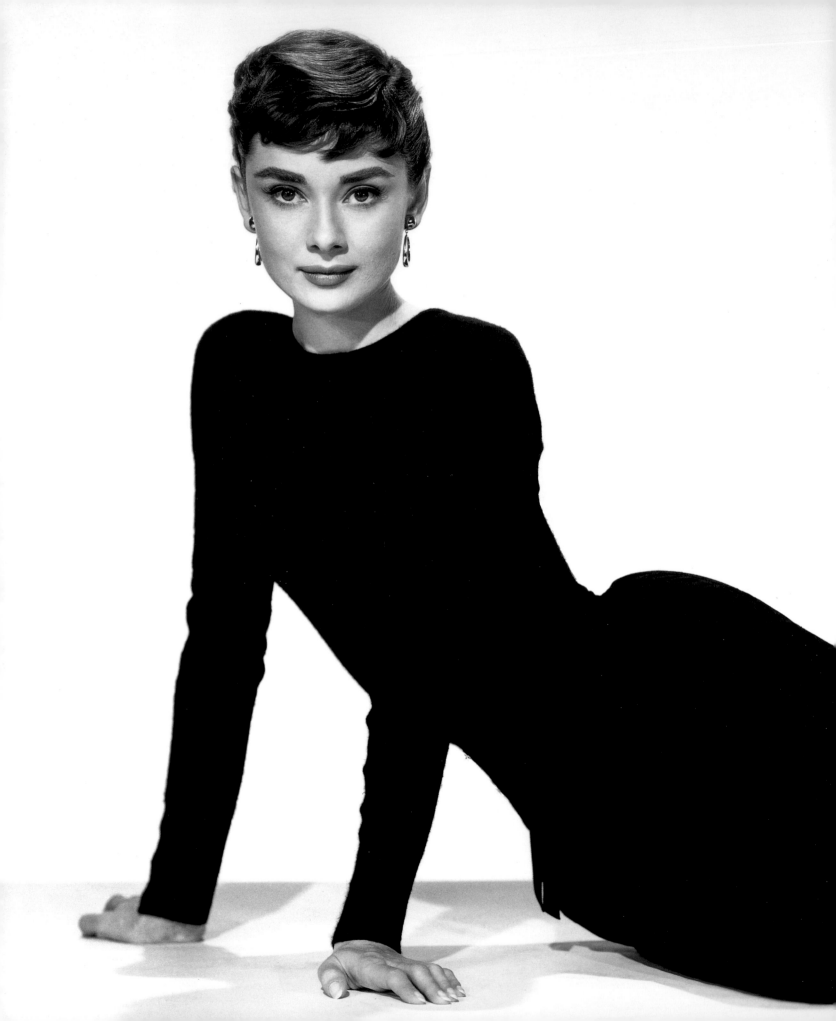

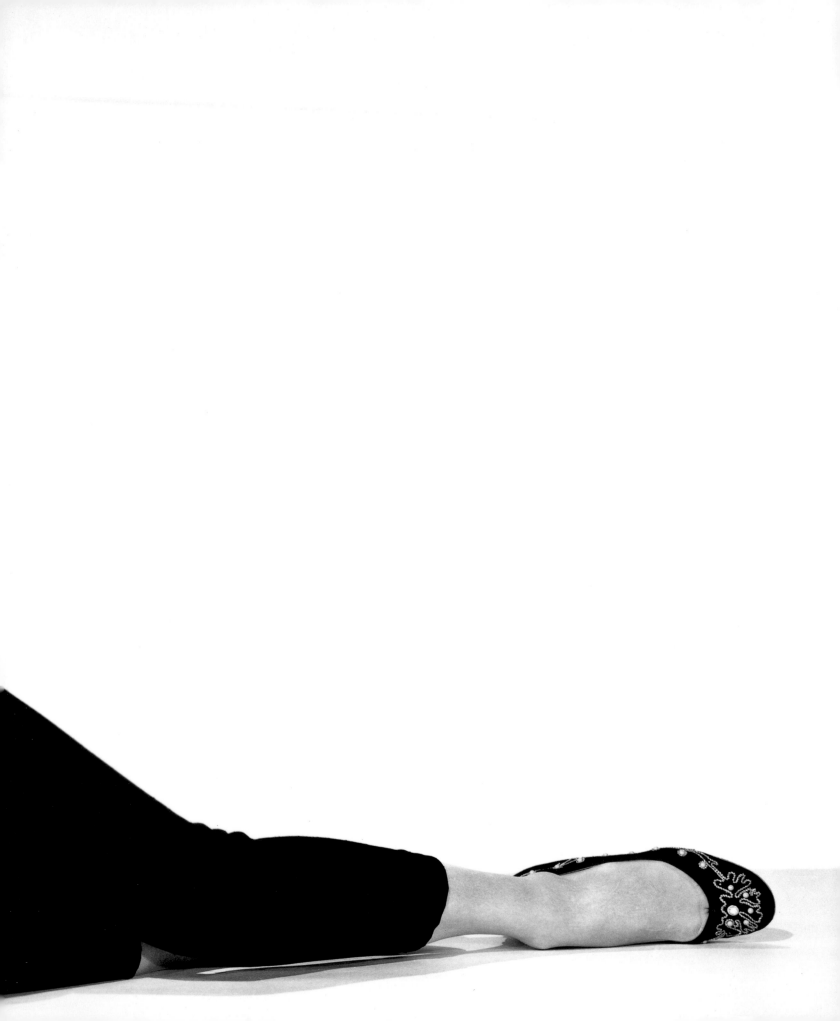

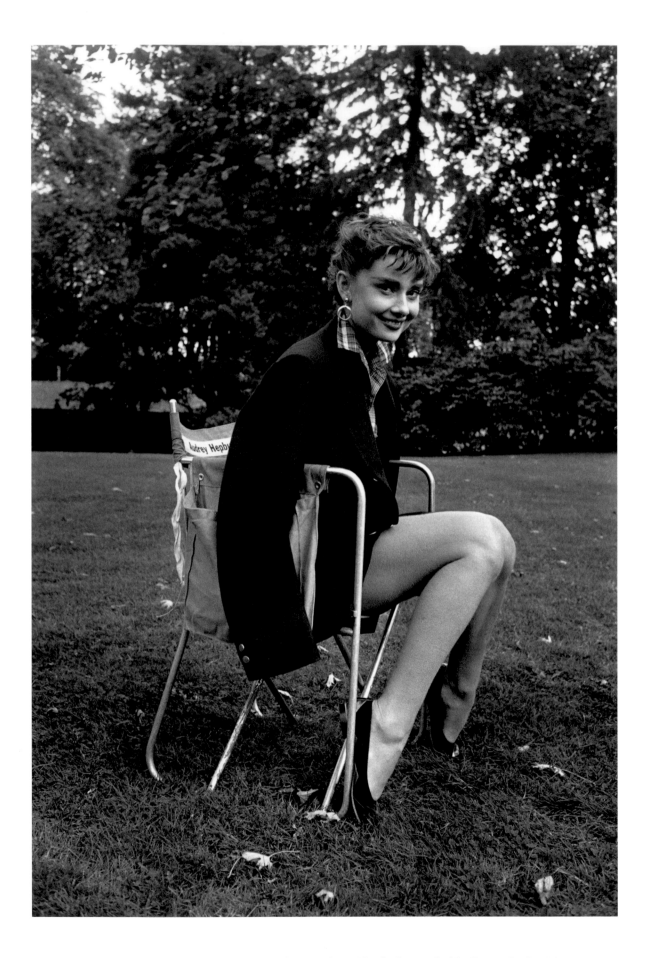

Audrey Hepburn during the shooting of 'Sabrina' in Long Island, photographed by Dennis Stock, 1953.

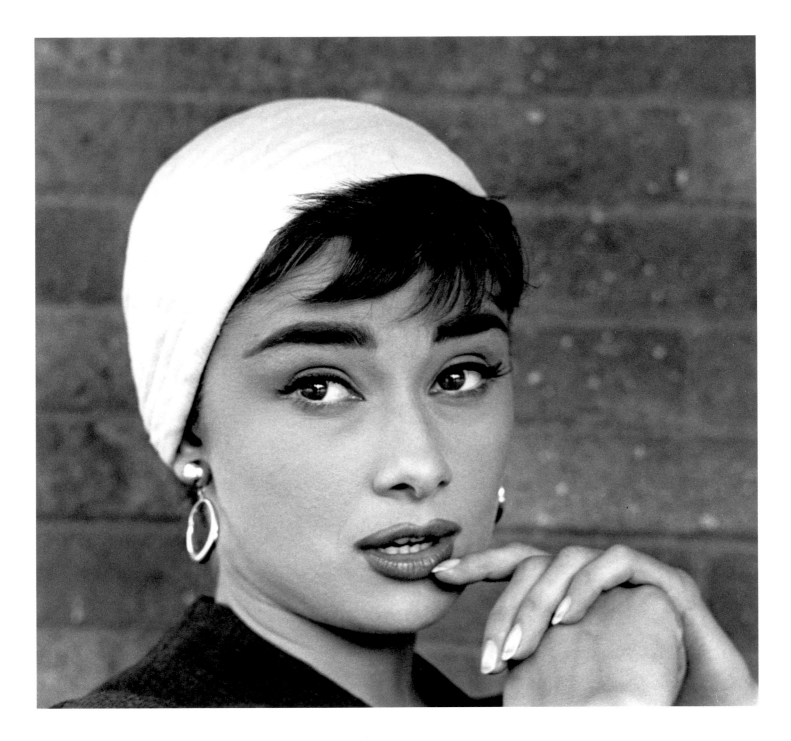

During the shooting of 'Sabrina', 1953. The once unprepossessing chauffeur's daughter has turned into a fashion-conscious and self-confident young woman with Parisian chic. Photo by Dennis Stock.

43

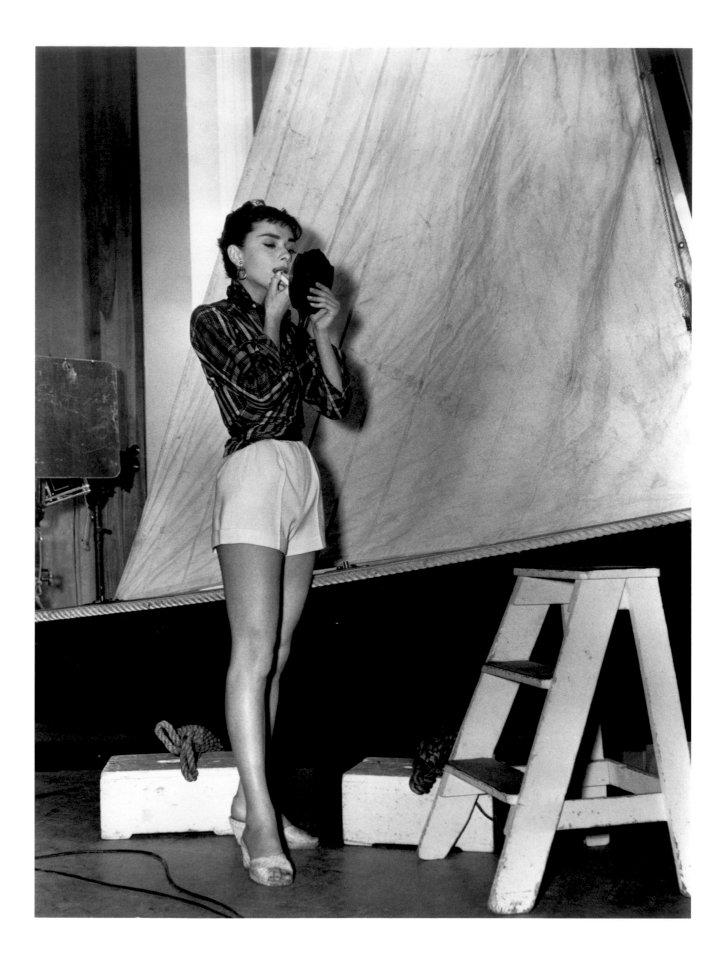

During the shooting of 'Sabrina', 1953.

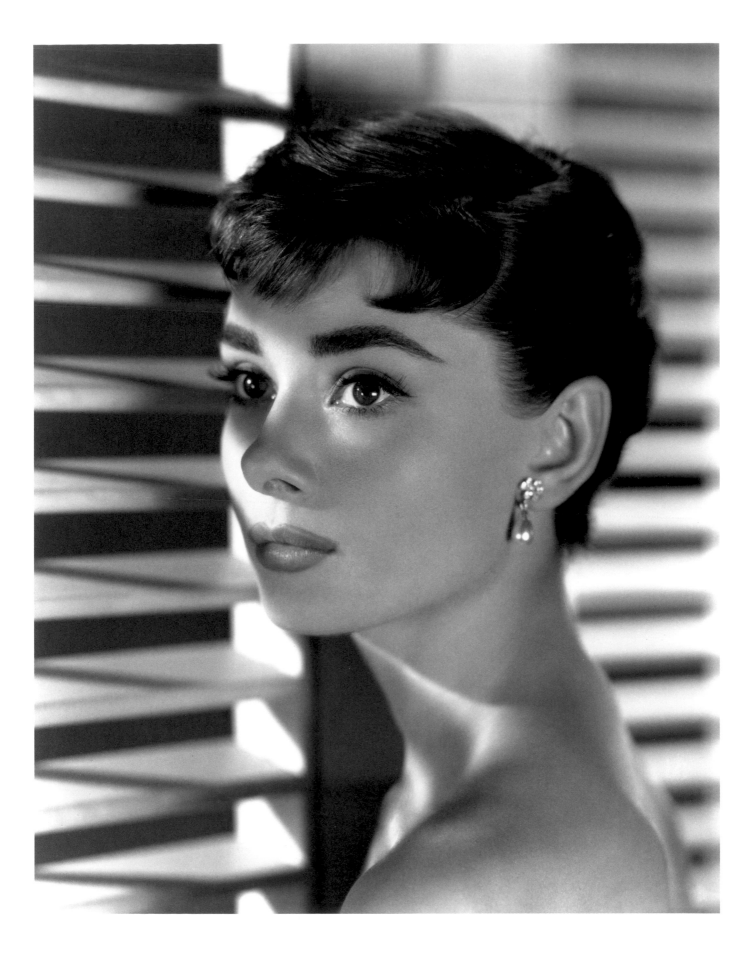

During the shooting of 'Sabrina', 1953.

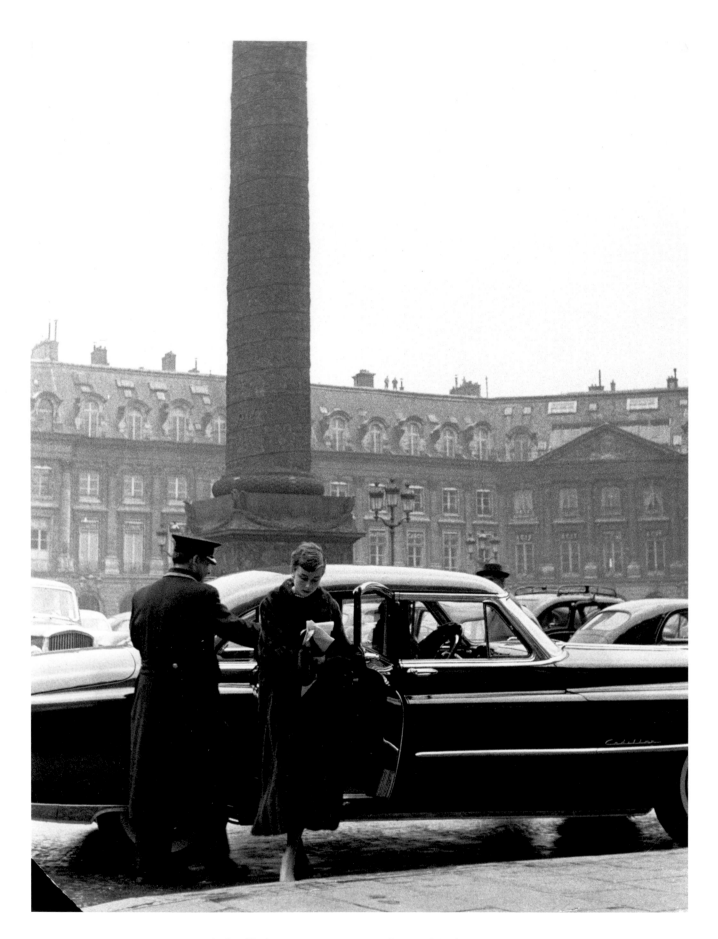

Audrey Hepburn on a private visit to Paris with Mel Ferrer, 1954.
Naturally, they stay at the Ritz on Place Vendôme.

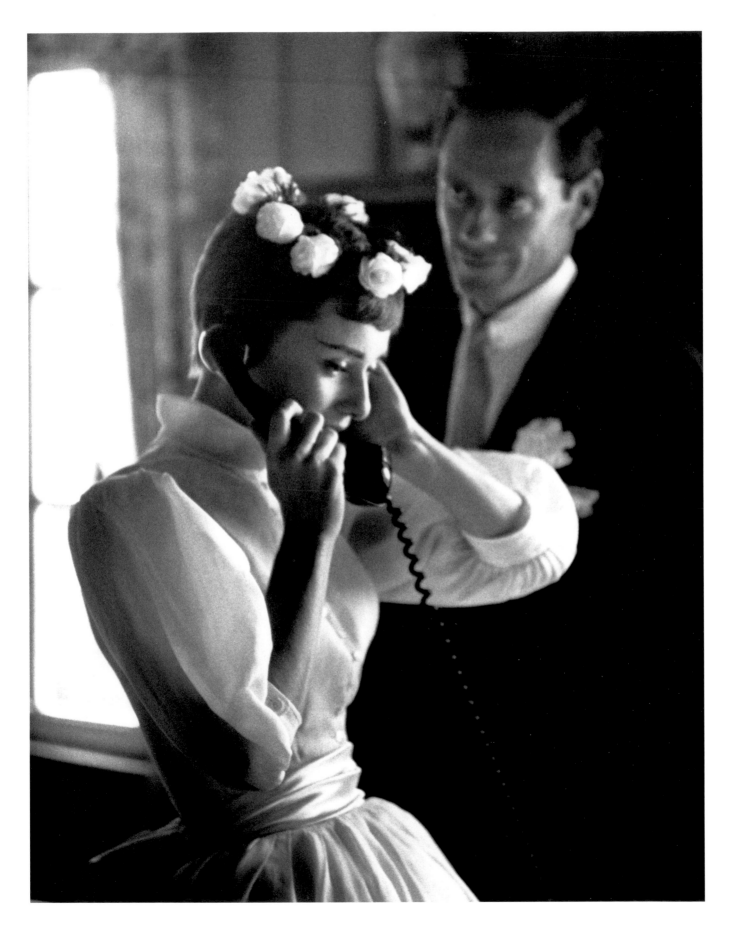

The wedding of the year, 1954. Audrey Hepburn and Mel Ferrer get married in Switzerland on 25 September. Photo by Ernst Haas for Magnum.

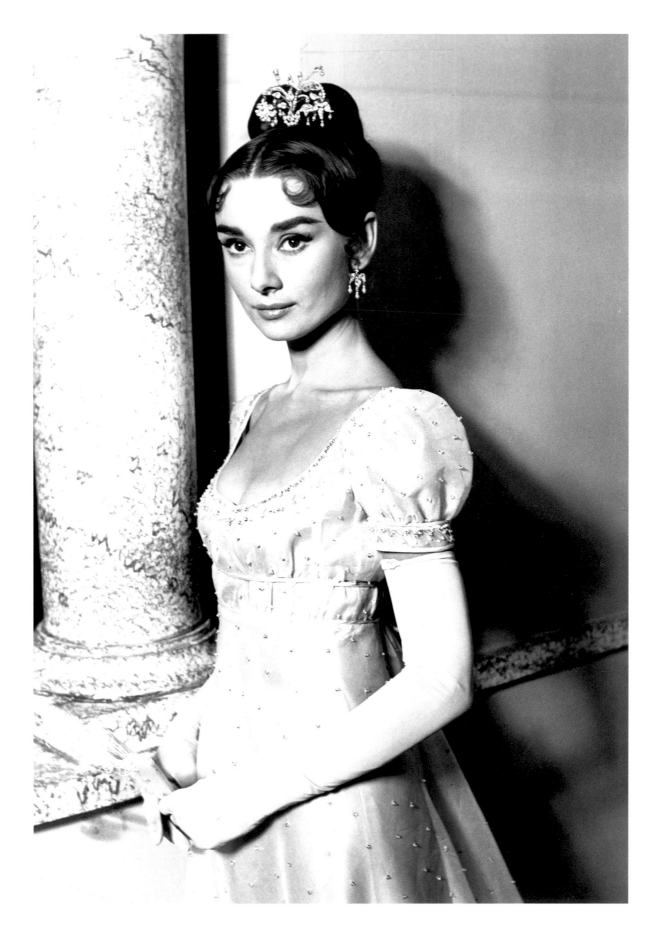

Alongside her husband, Mel Ferrer, and Henry Fonda, Audrey Hepburn plays Natasha in the wide-screen version of Tolstoy's novel 'War and Peace', 1955.

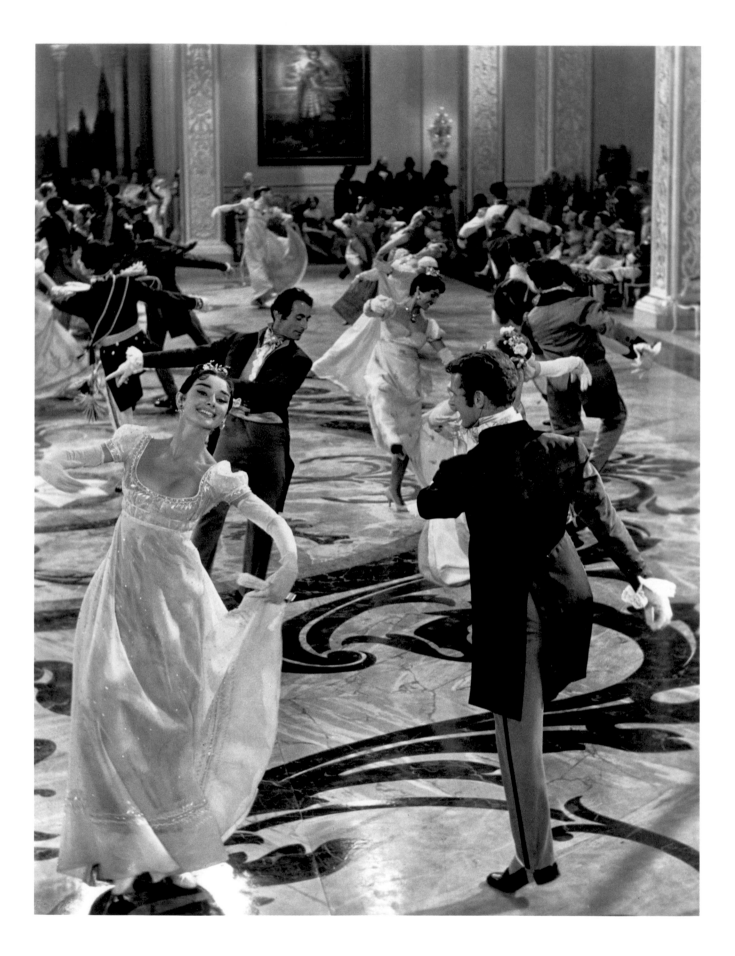

The grand ball scene in 'War and Peace'.

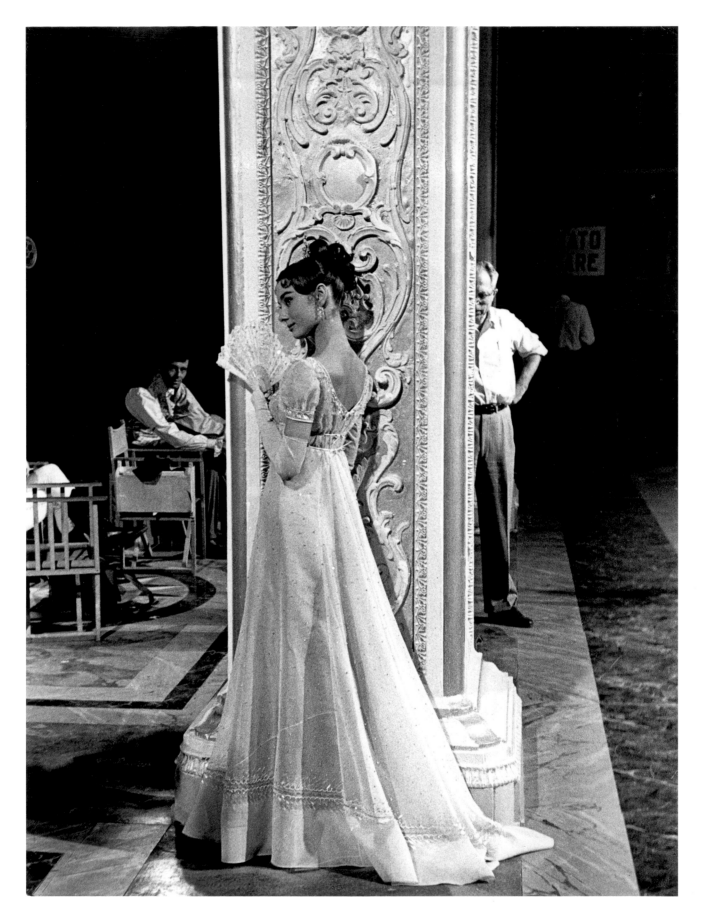

Natasha between two men: Henry Fonda, left, and director King Vidor during the shooting of
'War and Peace', 1955.

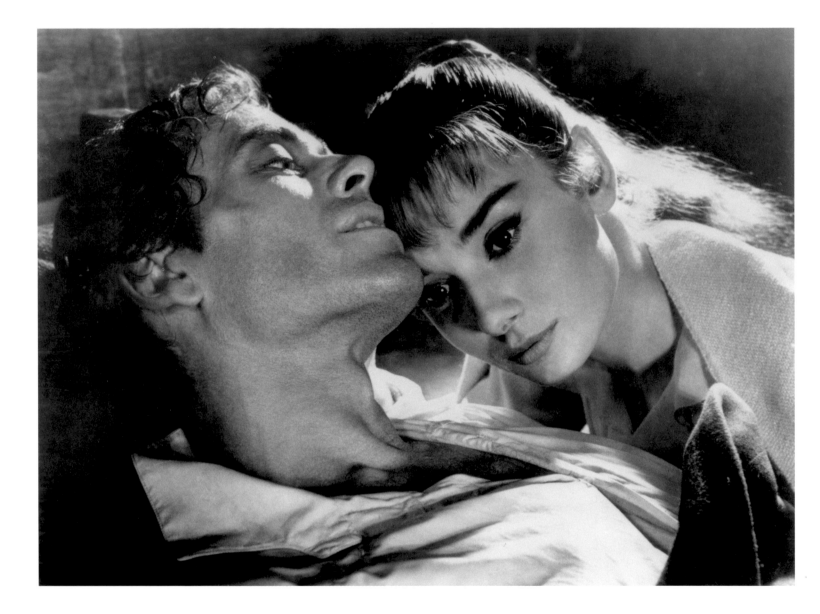

Shot with Mel Ferrer from 'War and Peace', 1955.

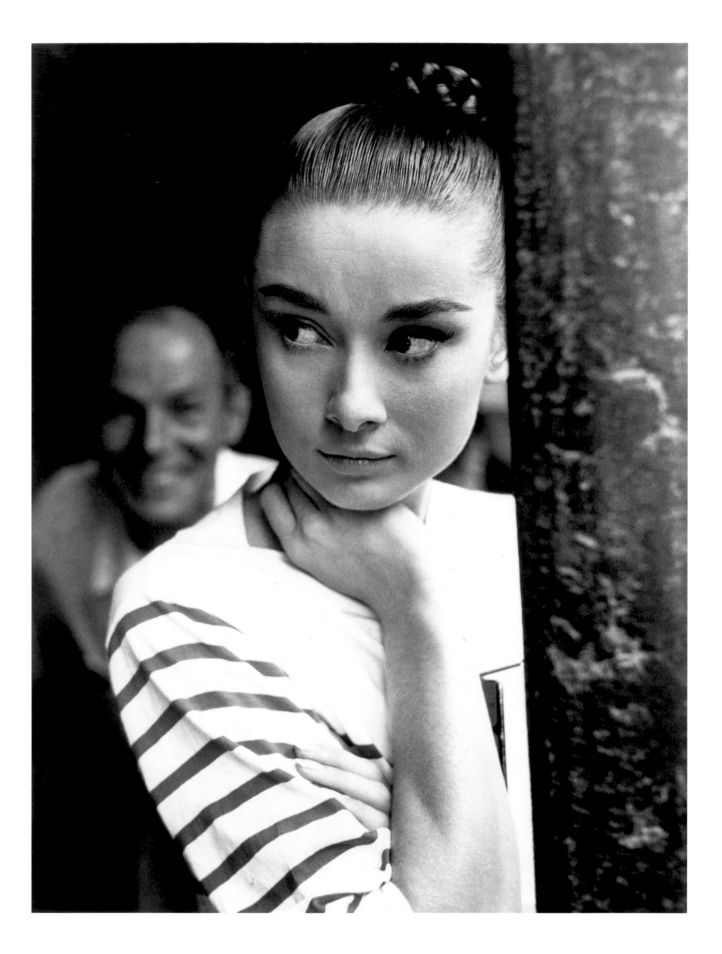

Portrait study during the shooting of 'War and Peace'. 53

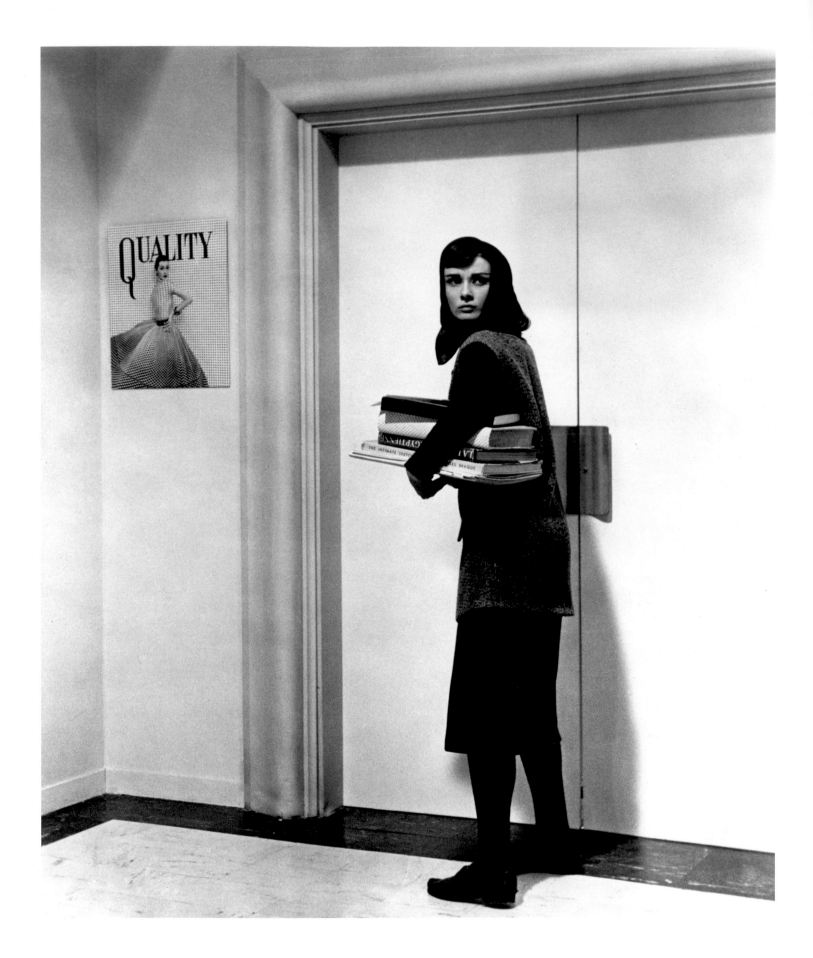

'Funny Face' before and after. The 'ugly duckling' becomes a stunningly beautiful model.

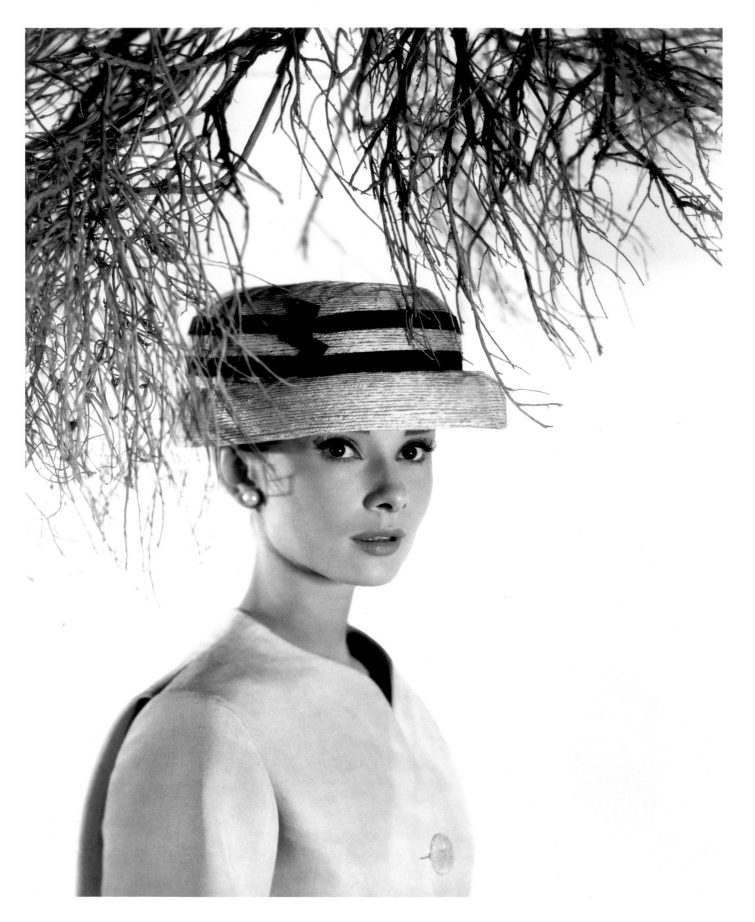

Bud Fraker photographed Audrey Hepburn in a Givenchy costume after her transformation, in a publicity still for 'Funny Face', 1956.

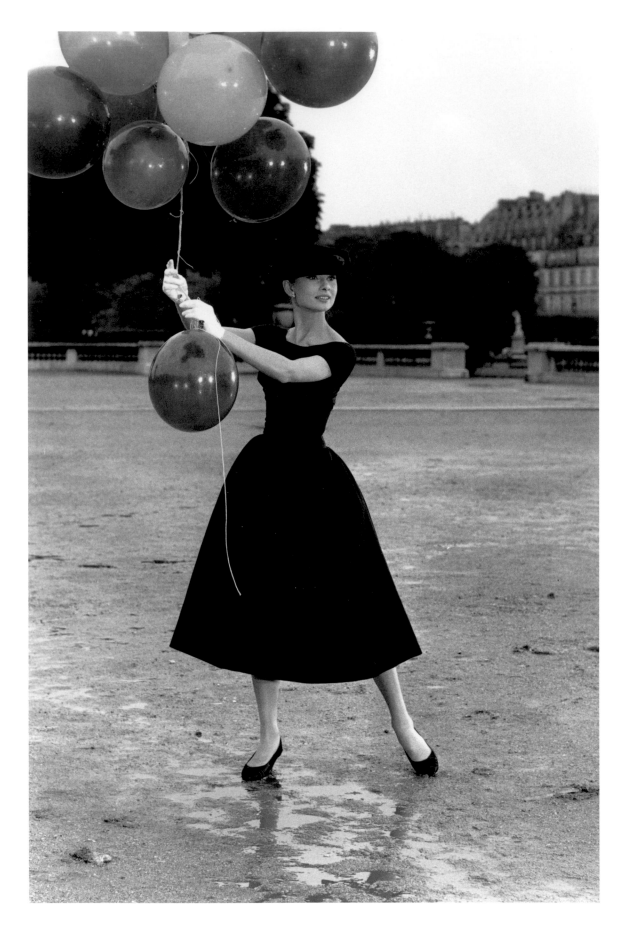

The fashion photos that play a central part in 'Funny Face' were arranged by no less a figure than Richard Avedon.

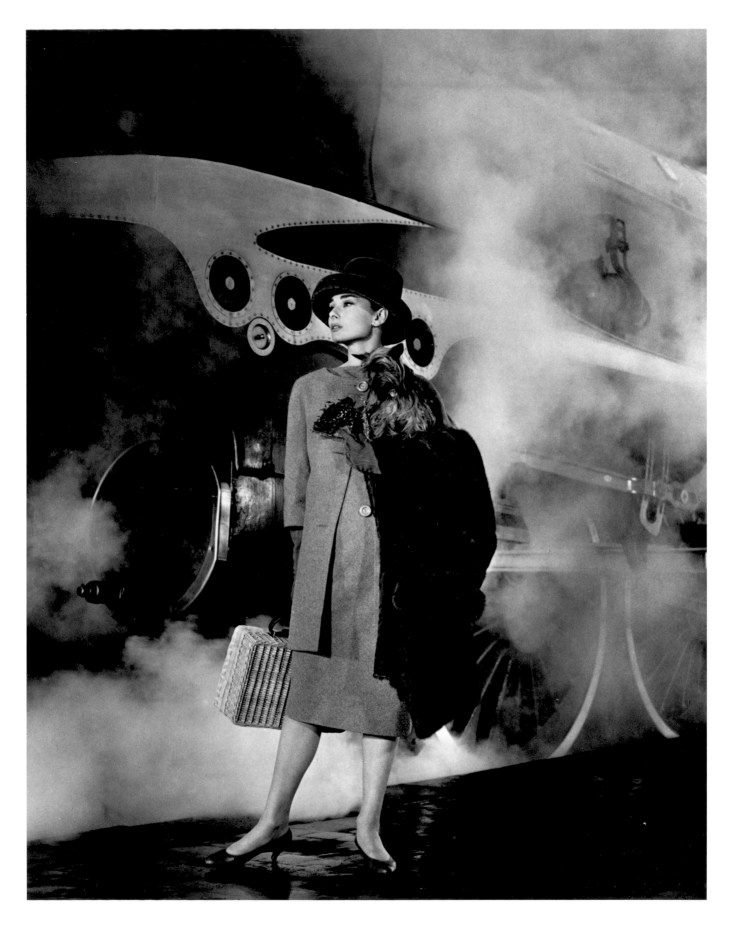

The picture on the left is by David Seymour, who was present on location while the film was being shot in Paris, and the one above is by Avedon.

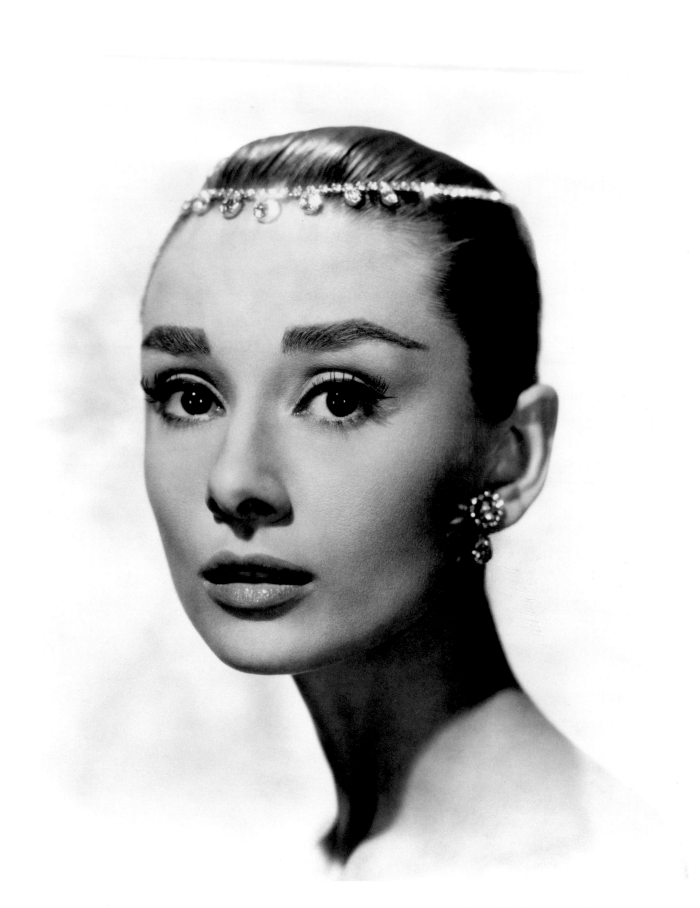

Portrait by Richard Avedon for 'Funny Face', 1956. For the first time, the 'little-girl look' gives way here to the film image of a more serious, starker beauty.

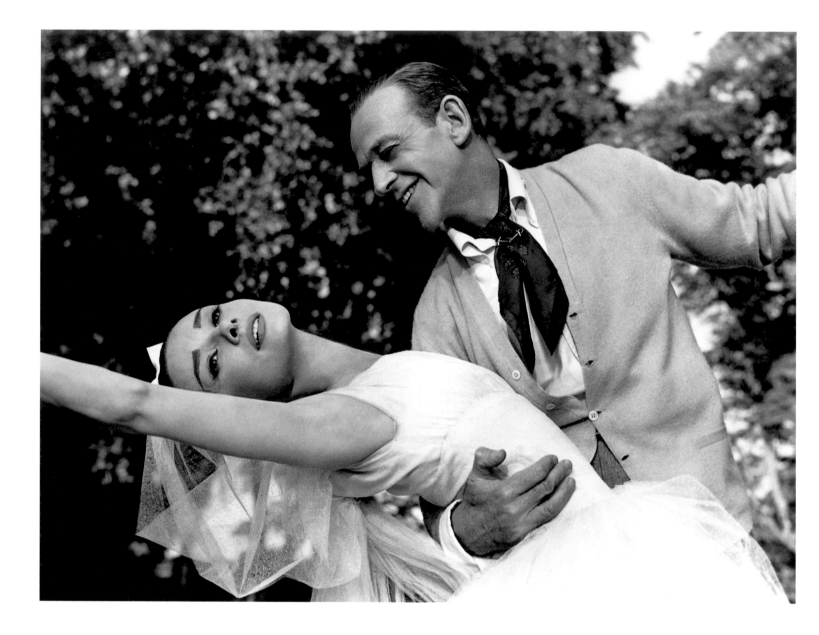

Fred Astaire, the idol of her youth, was Audrey's co-star in 'Funny Face'. Above, the happy ending in a
wedding dress, expressed through dance, of course.

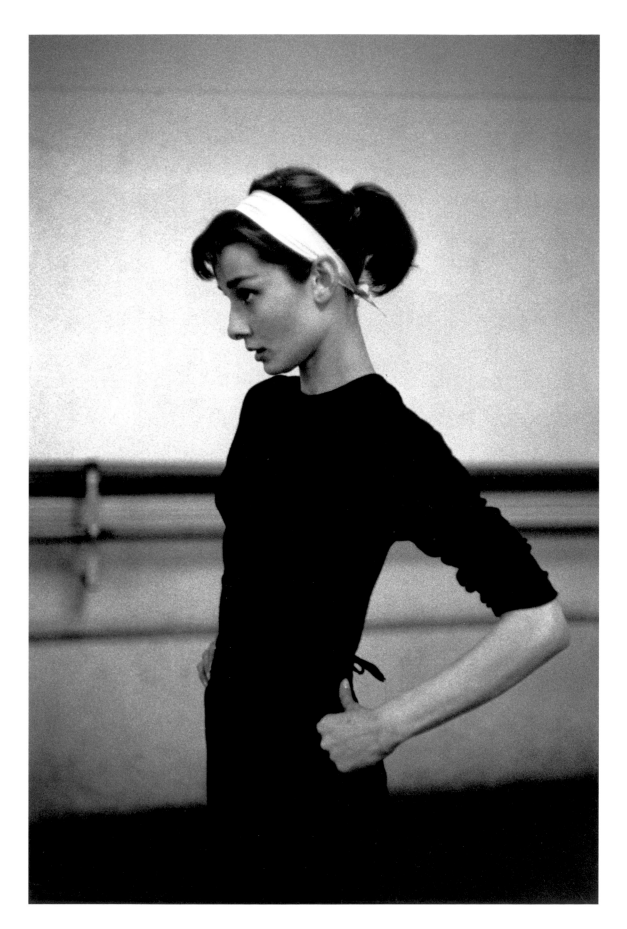

For the dance sequences in 'Funny Face', Audrey Hepburn once again studied ballet intensively.
Photo by David Seymour.

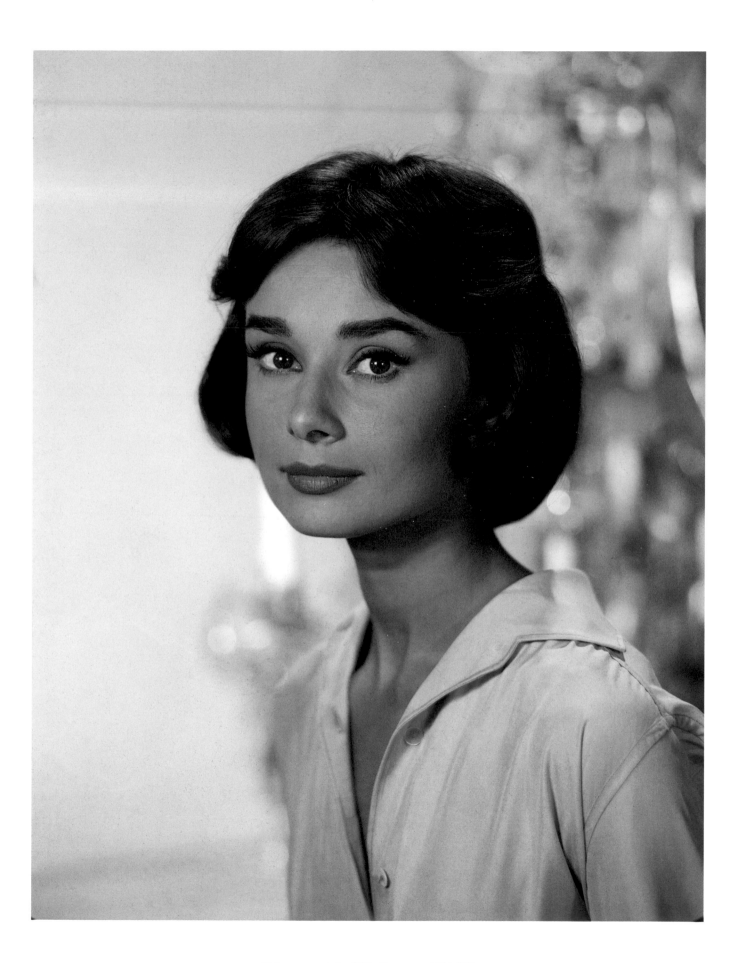

Colour portrait by Willy Rizzo, ca. 1956 / 57.

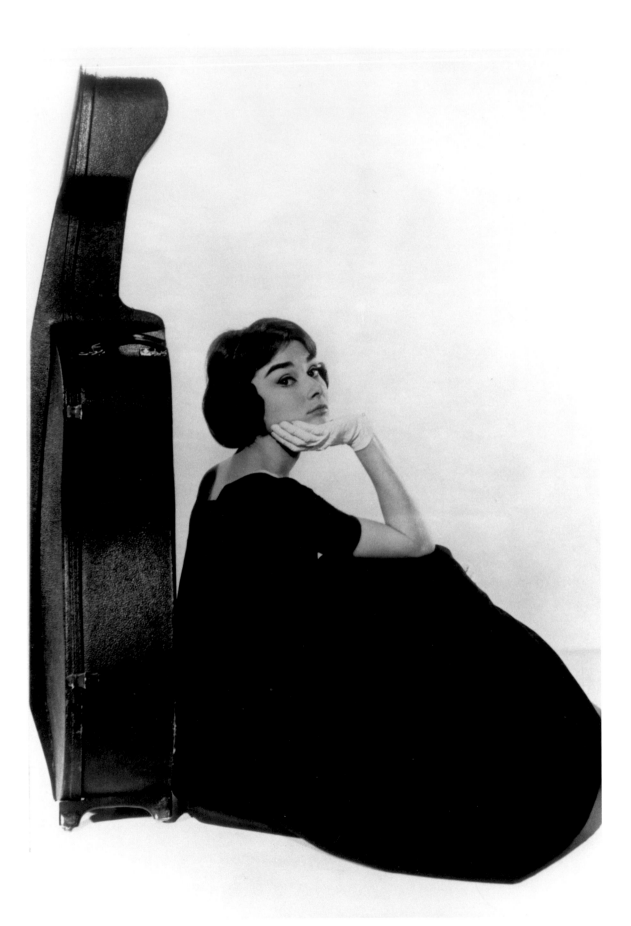

'Love in the Afternoon', Billy Wilder's second film with Audrey Hepburn, is once again set in Paris.
A publicity still, with the awkward cello that causes all sorts of problems.

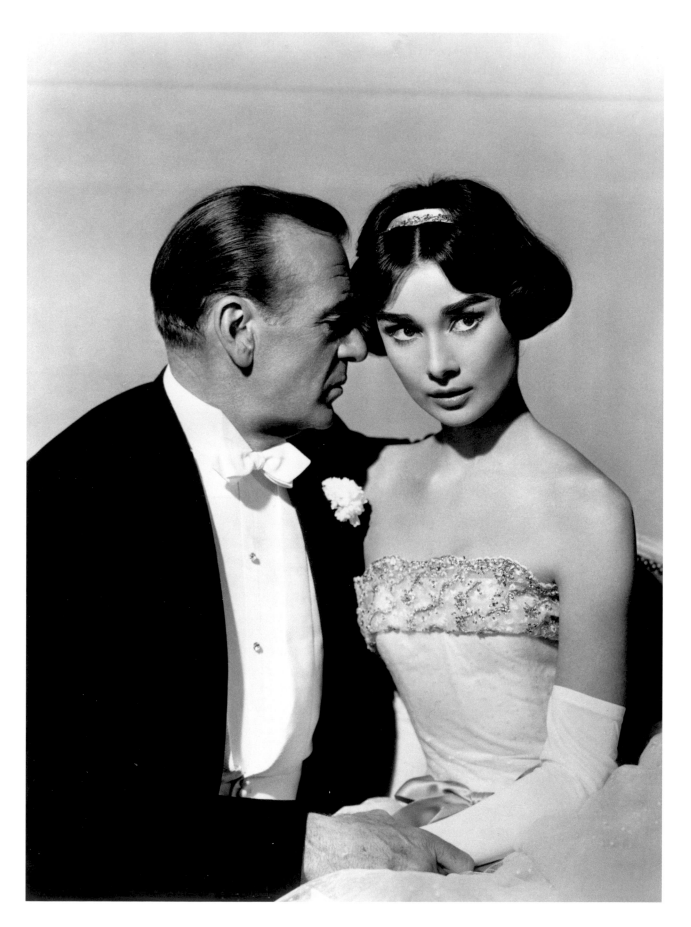

*Ariane, a student at the conservatory, falls in love with a rich American, played by Gary Cooper,
who is naturally staying at the Ritz.*

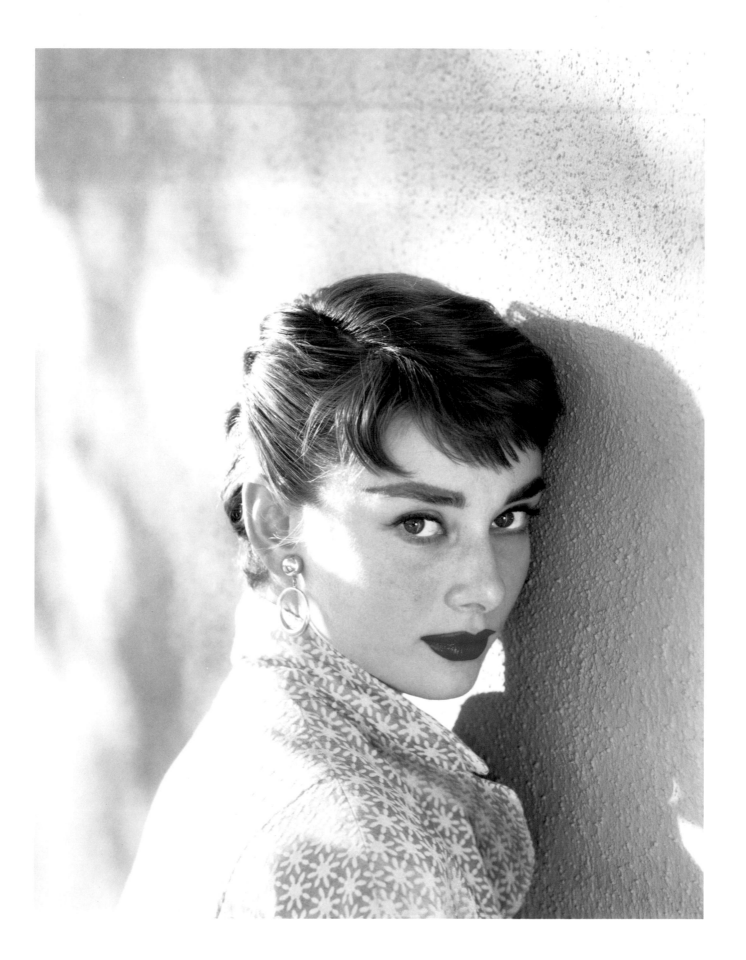

Cinderella is gradually growing up. Portrait study by John Engstead, ca. 1954.

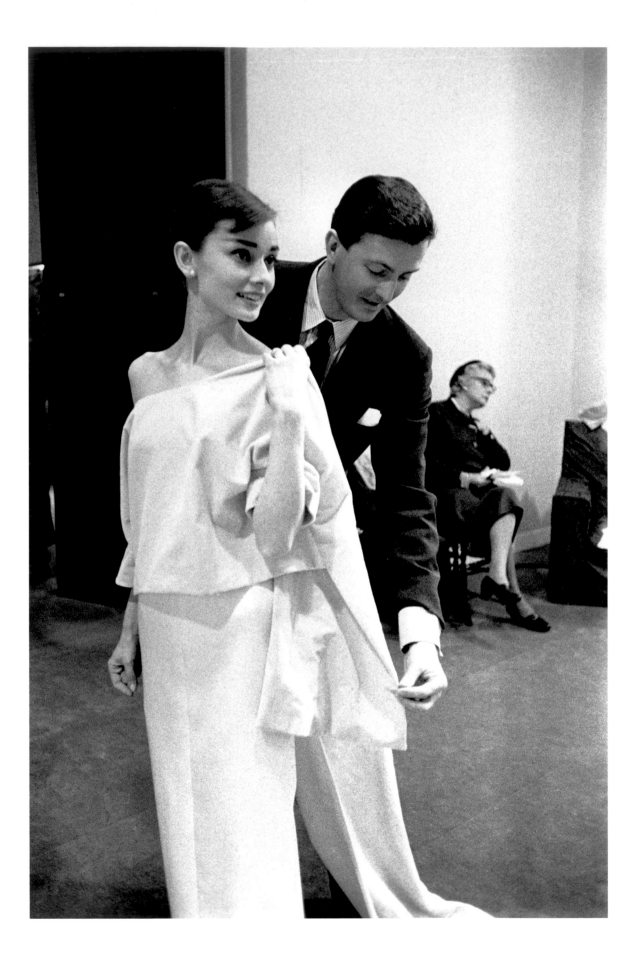

Audrey Hepburn with 'her' couturier, Hubert de Givenchy. Photo by David Seymour, 1956.

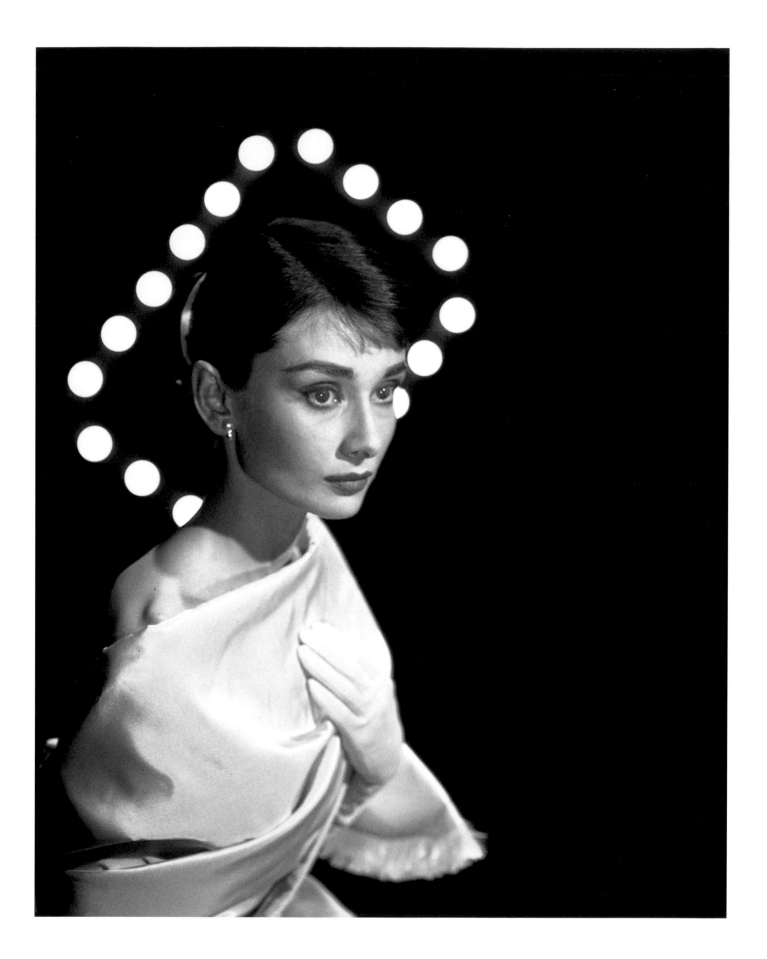

Fashion shot, ca. 1956.

Hollywood director Fred Zinnemann puts Audrey Hepburn on screen in a serious character part for the first time. An obviously more mature Audrey, with her terrier 'Famous' in her lap, during shooting for 'The Nun's Story', 1958.

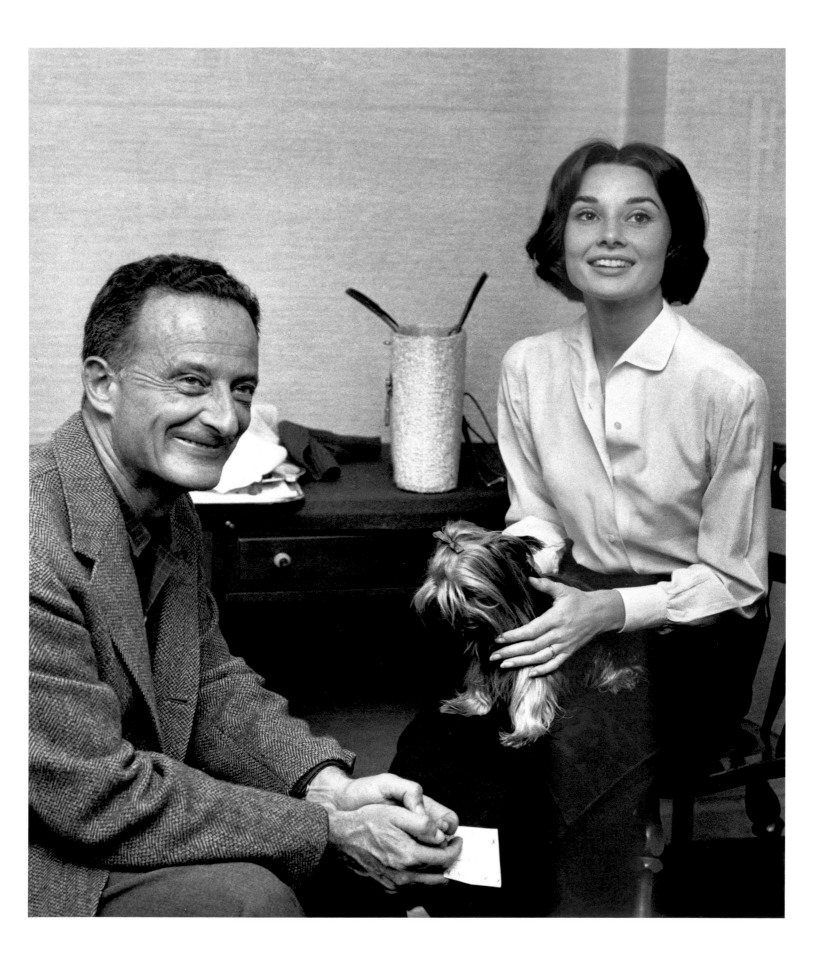

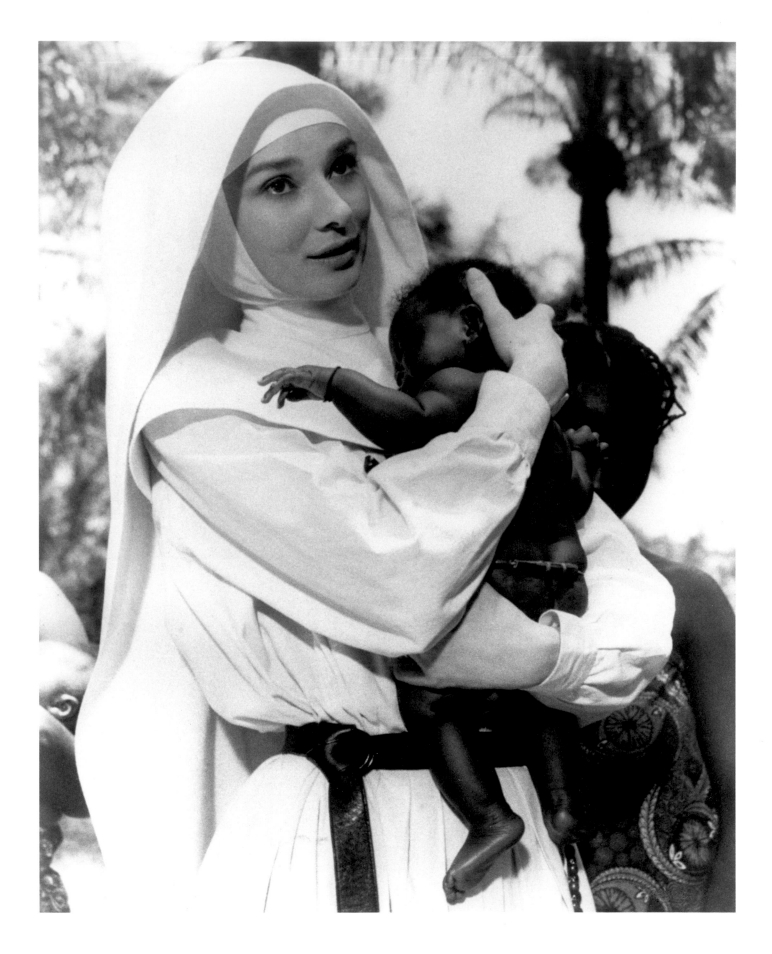

Audrey Hepburn as Sister Lukas in 'The Nun's Story', at one of the order's mission stations in Africa.

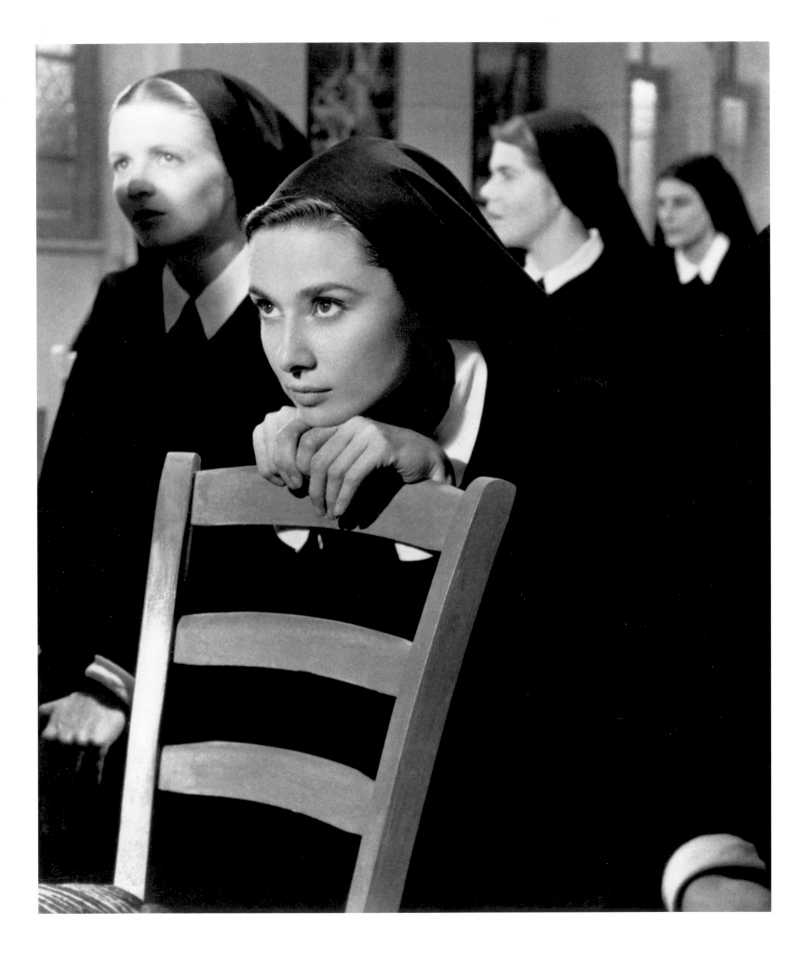

In the Belgian convent, as a novice plagued by doubts.

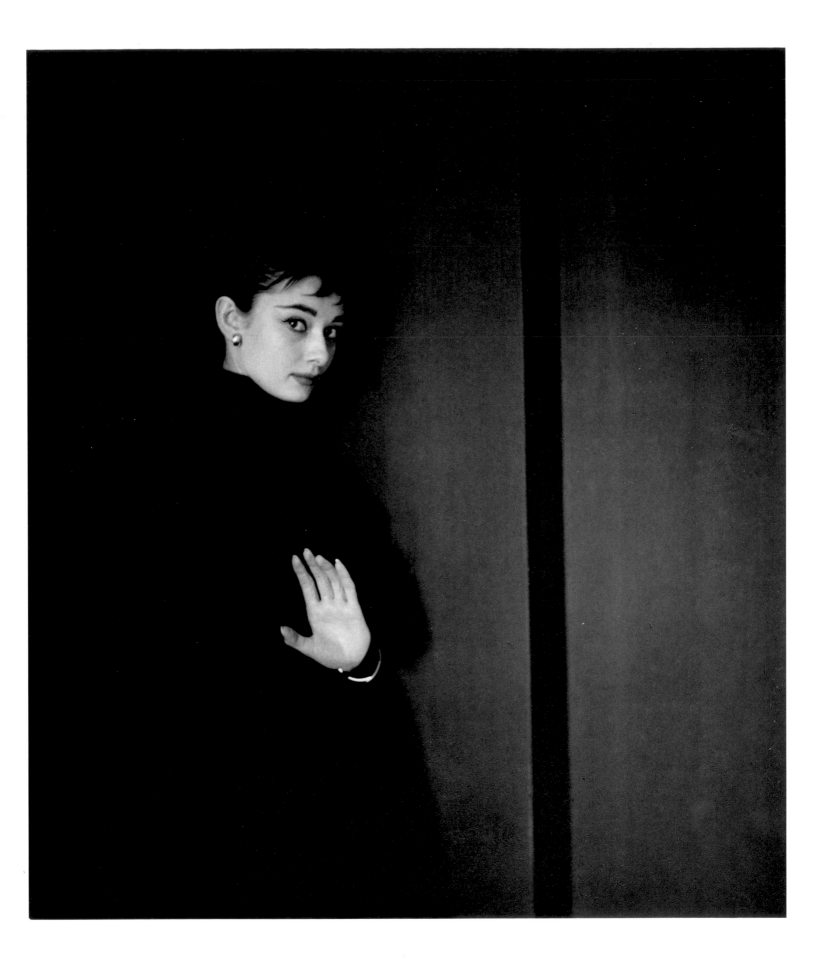

Portrait by Cecil Beaton, 1958.

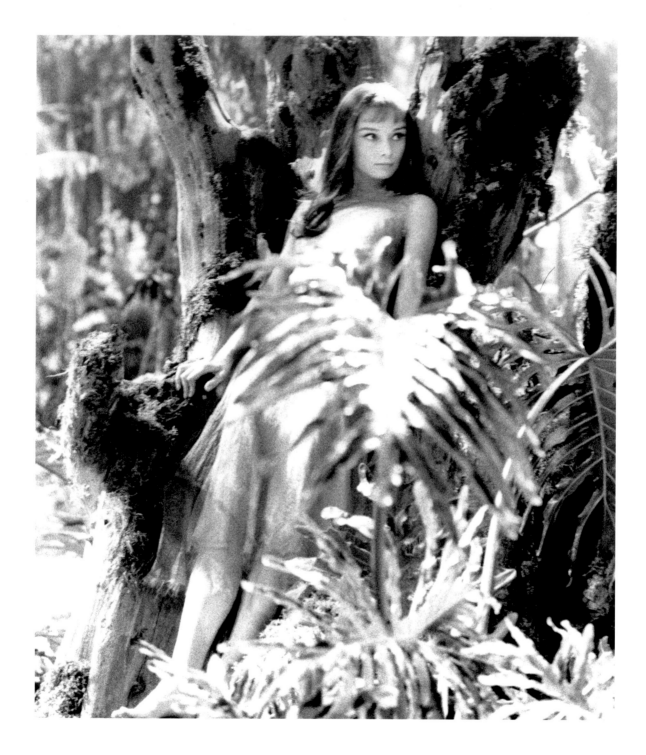

Mel Ferrer directed the colour film 'Green Mansions', in which Audrey Hepburn played Rima, the jungle girl. The MGM production was not particularly successful, and Ferrer was accused of having used the film merely as an excuse to show his wife in a favourable light in endless wide-screen close-ups. The photo above is by Bob Willoughby.

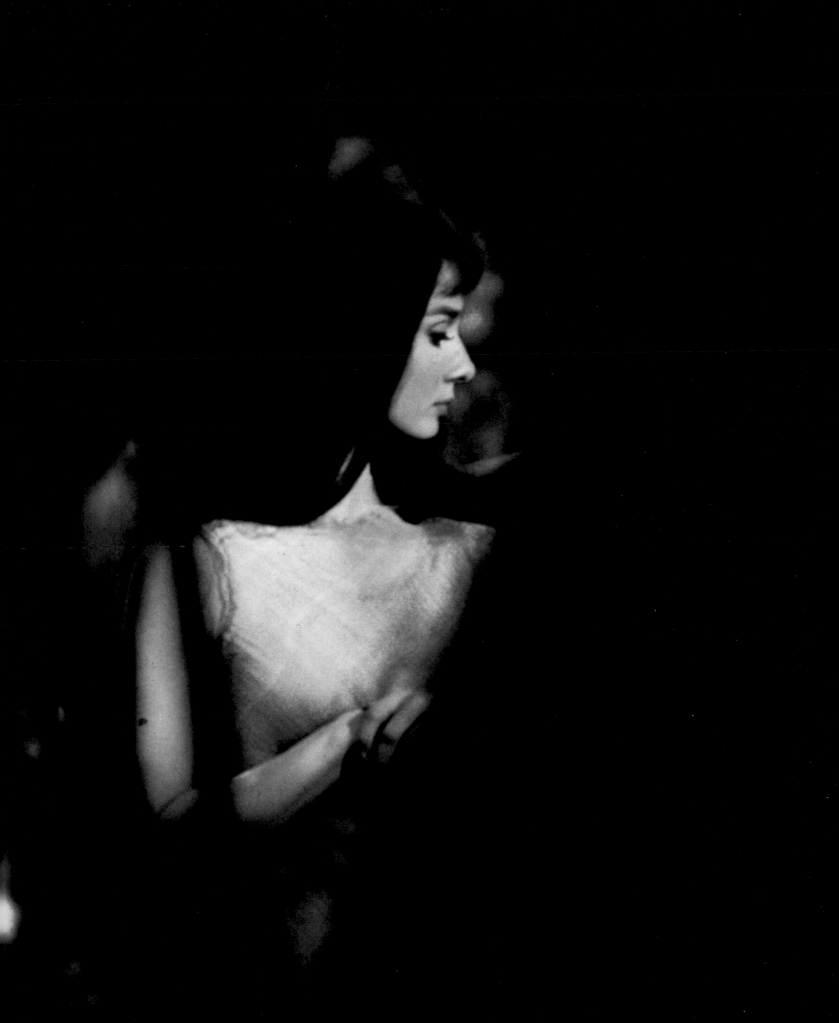

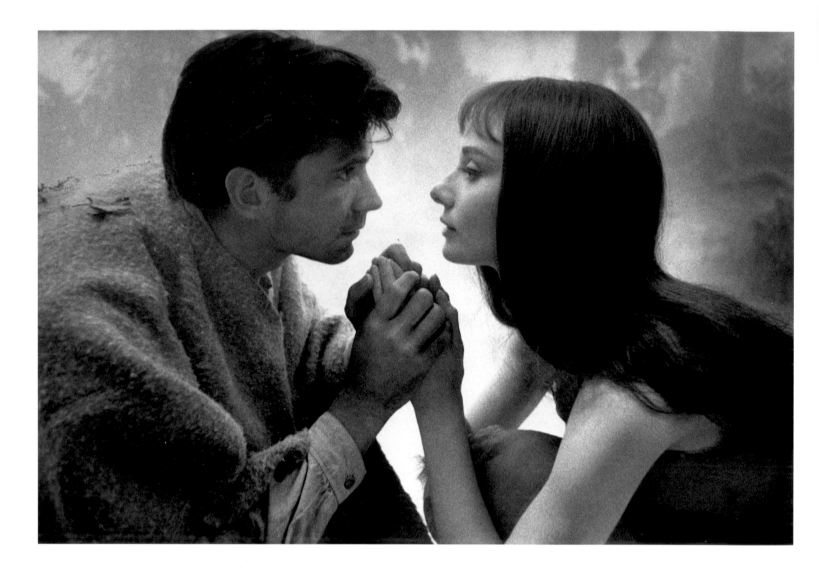

In 'Green Mansions', Anthony Perkins falls in love with Rima, the child of nature who is destroyed by contact with civilization. Film still by Bob Willoughby.

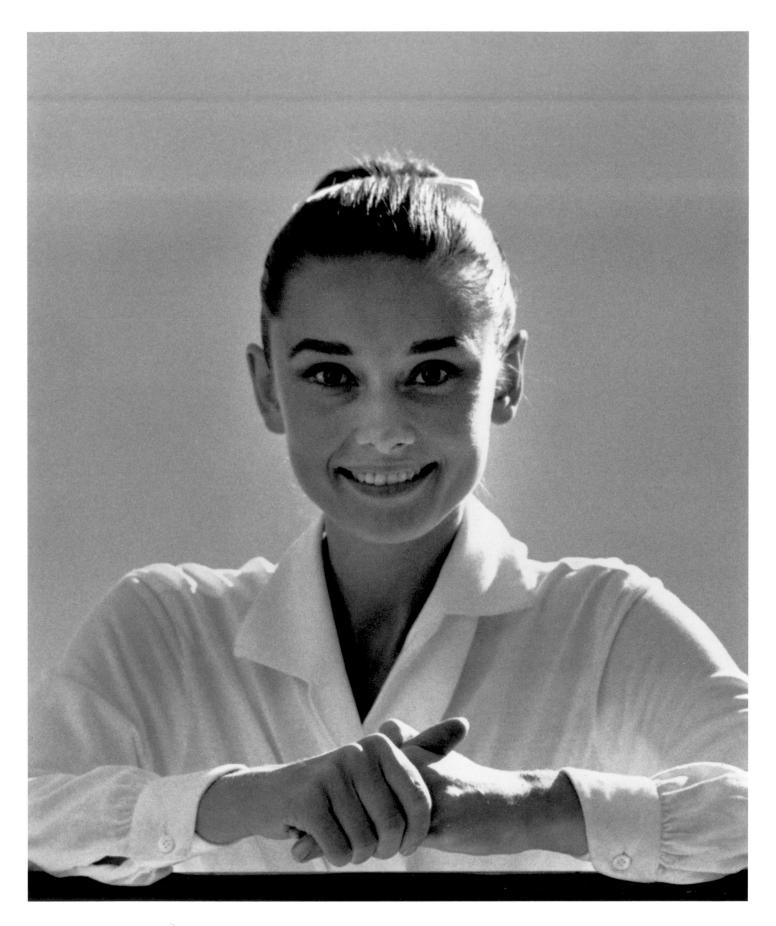

This portrait, by Inge Morath, was taken in Mexico in 1959 during the shooting of John Huston's 'The Unforgiven', Audrey Hepburn's only western.

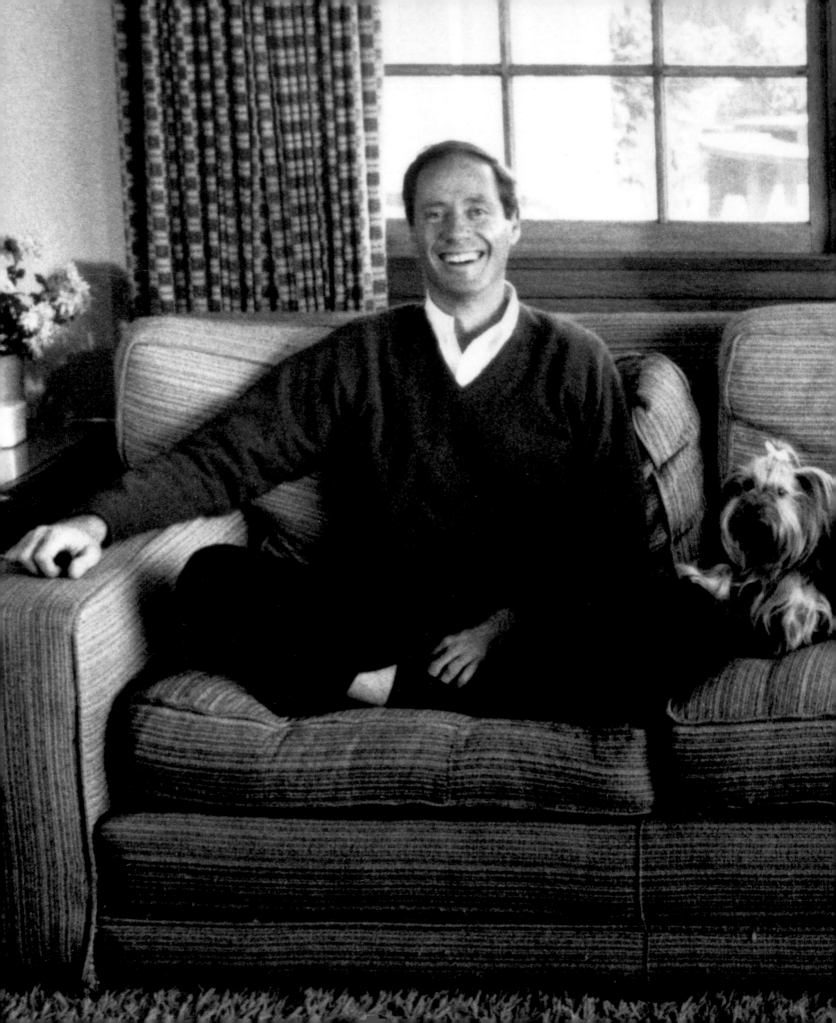

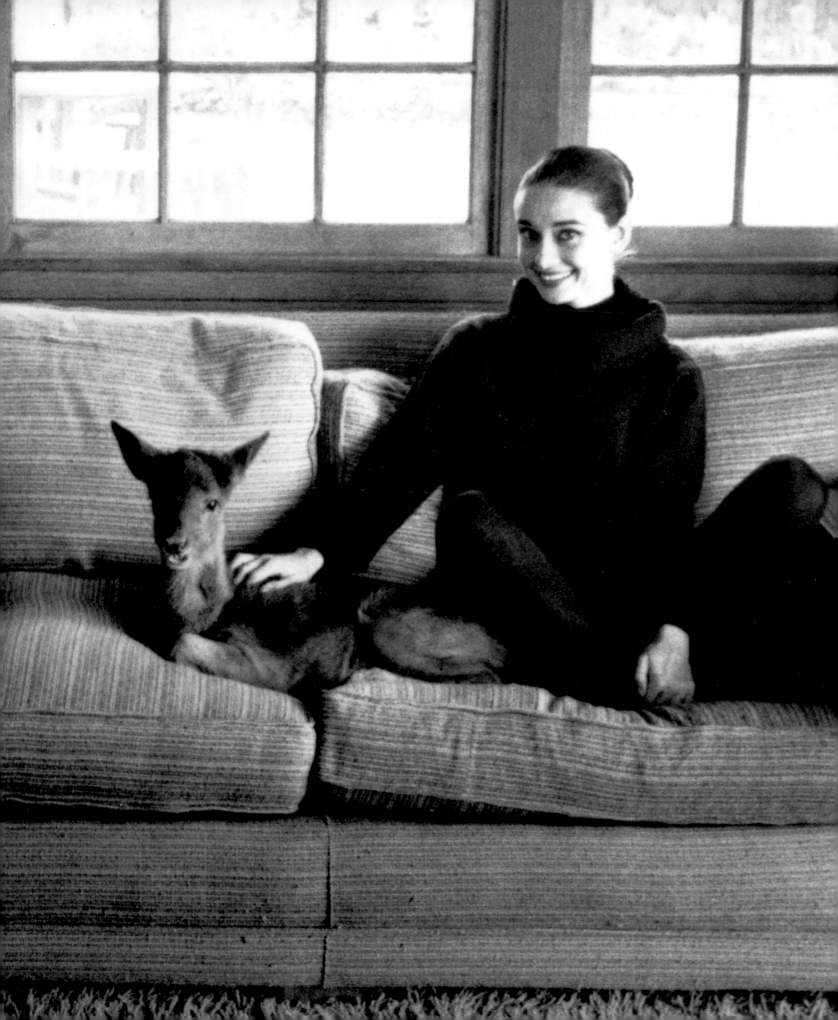

Preceding two pages:
Bob Willoughby took this double portrait with pets in Ferrer and Hepburn's Swiss home in Bürgenstock.
The couple used the photo on their private Christmas card in 1958. The tame fawn had played an
important part in 'Green Mansions'.

'Breakfast at Tiffany's, the film version of the viciously satirical story by Truman Capote, is the film
that had the most lasting impact on Audrey Hepburn's screen image. Here she is seen with co-star
George Peppard studying Tiffany's shop window. Film still, 1960.

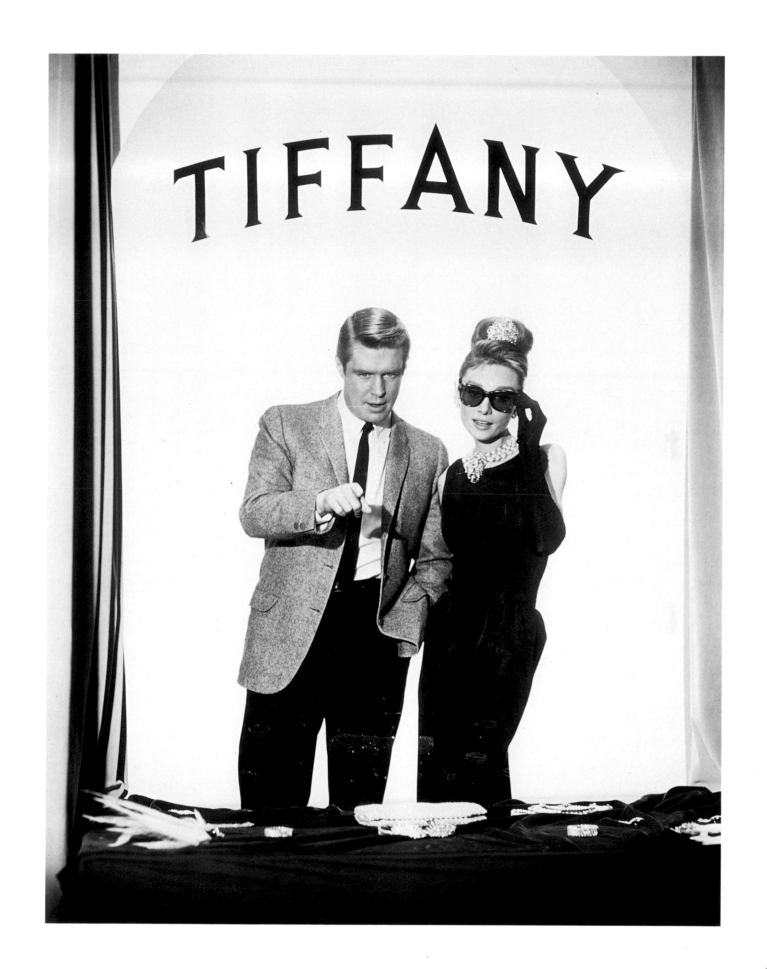

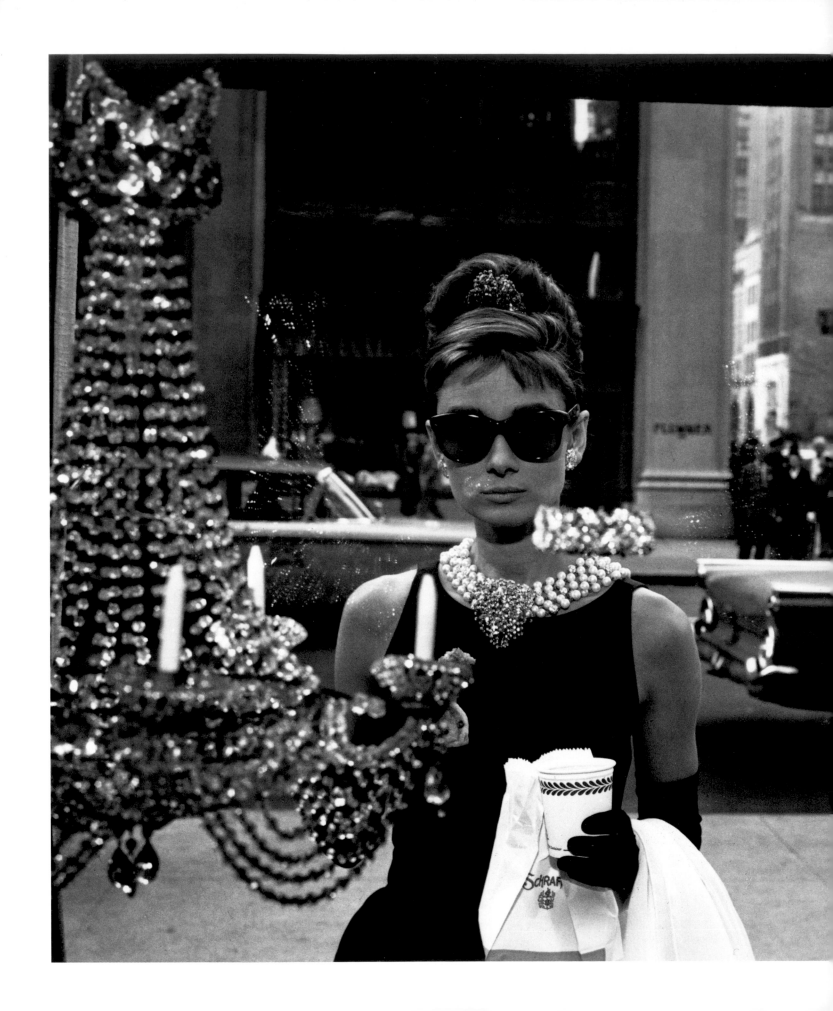

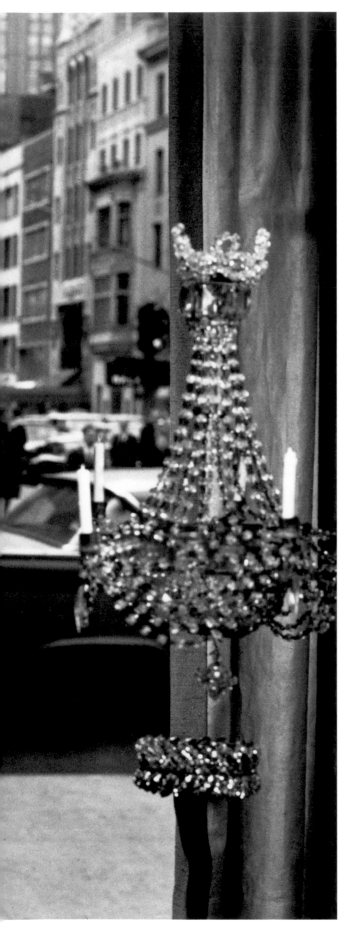

The breakfast in question takes place
on the other side of the jewel-studded shop window,
and consists of a hamburger. Audrey Hepburn
became the fashion idol of the early 1960s
as Holly Golightly, in a black dress
with big black sunglasses and imitation
diamonds.

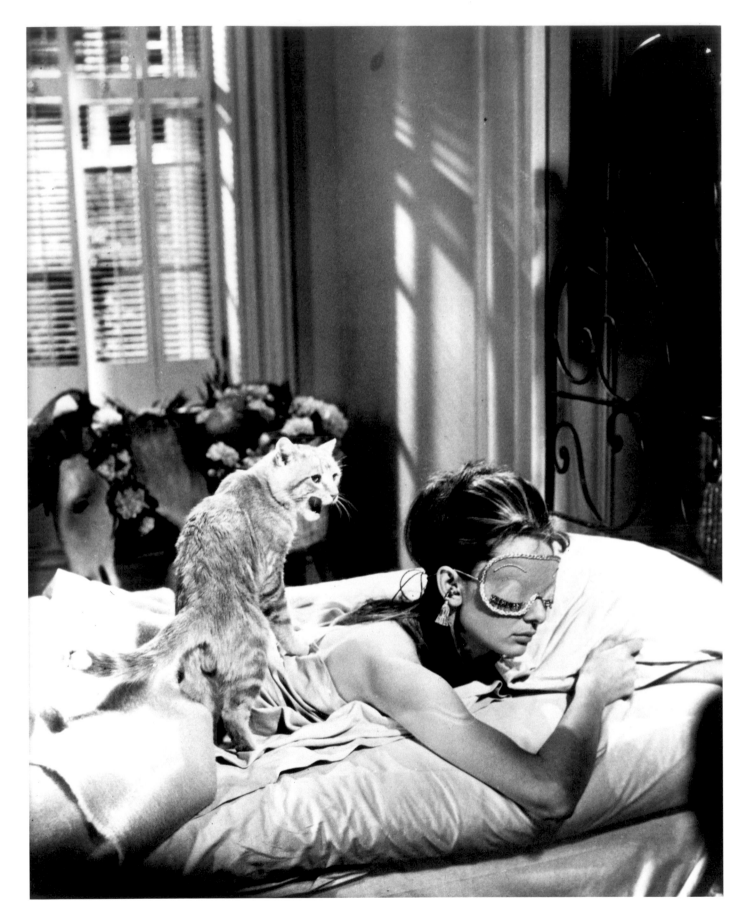

The anonymous cat has a fateful role to play towards the end of 'Breakfast at Tiffany's'. Here it is ruining Holly's attempt to recover from a raging hangover.

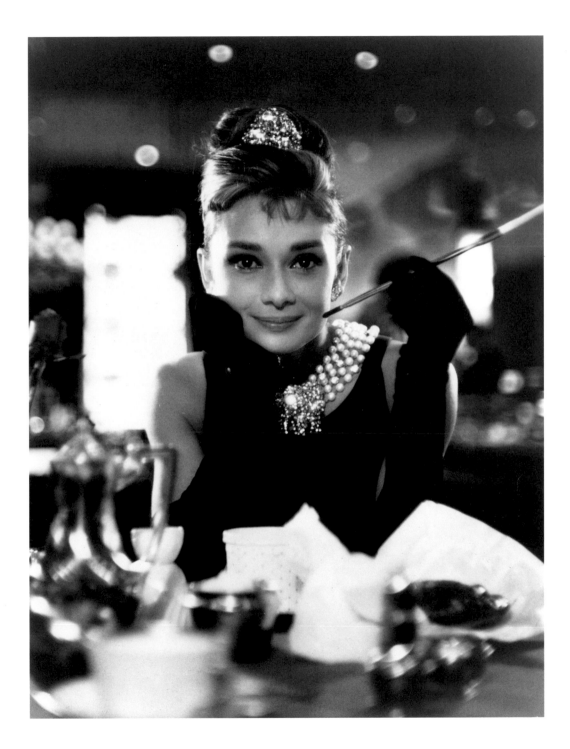

Audrey Hepburn as everyone knows her, more endearing than disreputable as Miss Golightly,
with a cigarette-holder and long gloves. Publicity still.

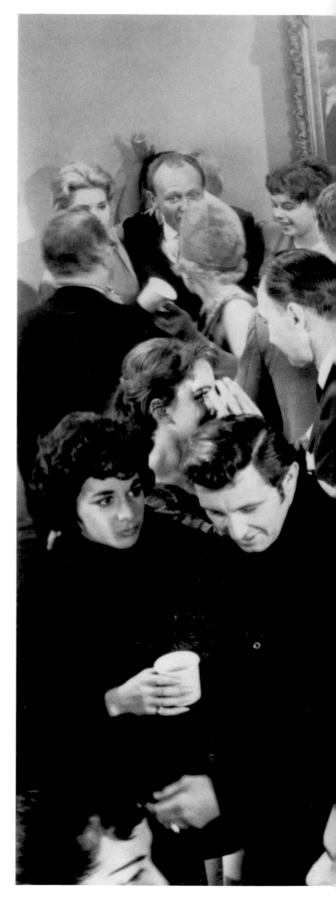

The New York society hostess in full action. Among her eccentric
party guests, Holly is apparently chic; later, without her makeup and rather lonely,
she sits at the kitchen window and sings 'Moon River' to guitar accompaniment.
The song received an Oscar.

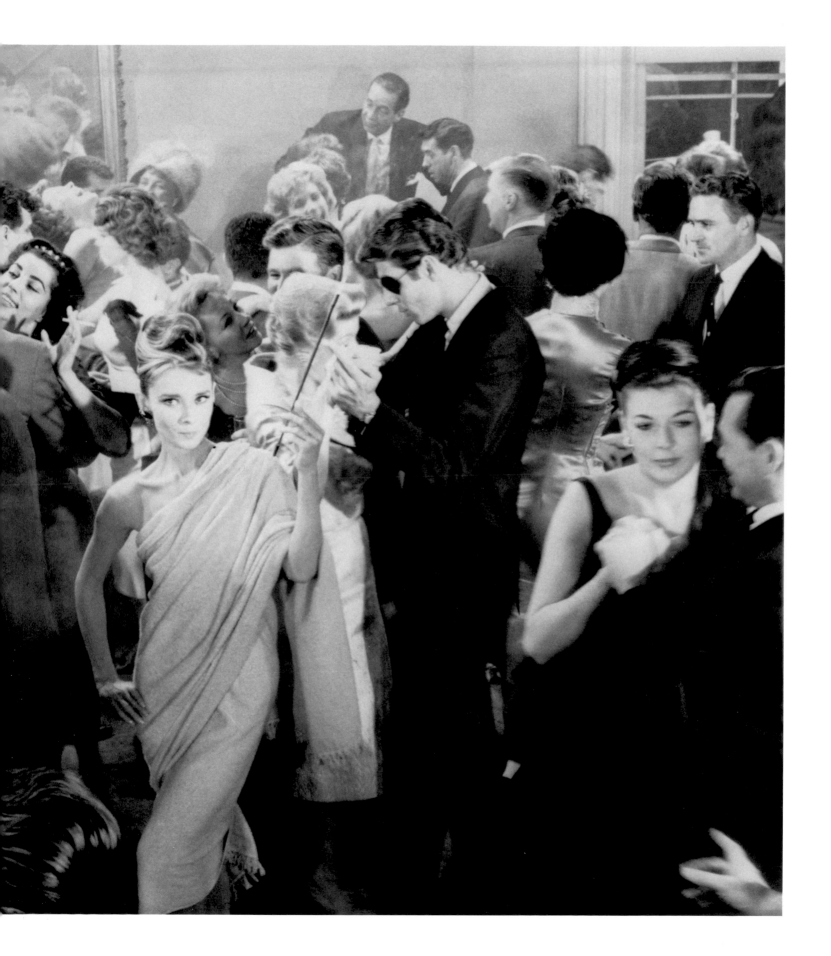

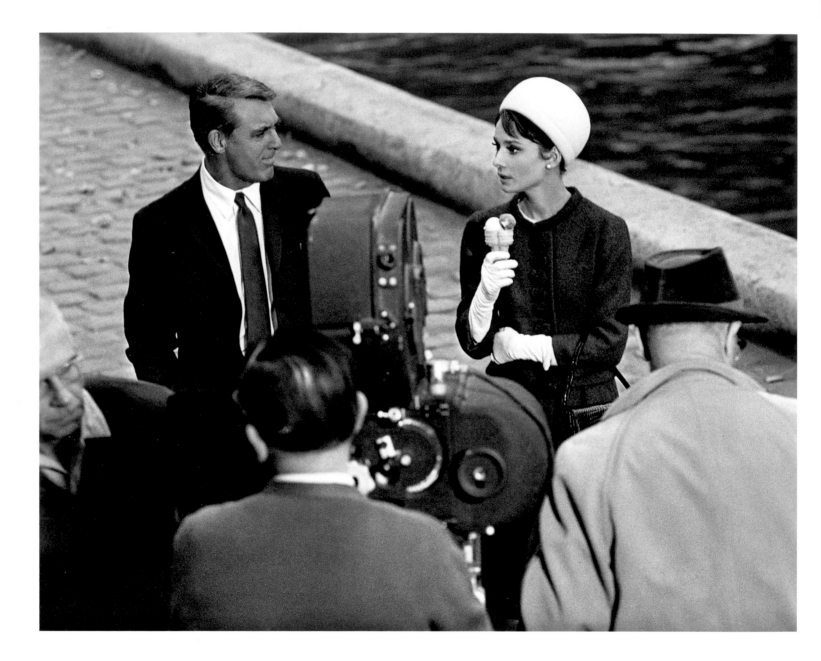

Stanley Donen's gangster thriller 'Charade' was applauded for its 'Hitchcock quality'. Audrey Hepburn,
looking extremely elegant in the latest Givenchy collection, with her co-star Cary Grant during shooting
in Paris in 1962.

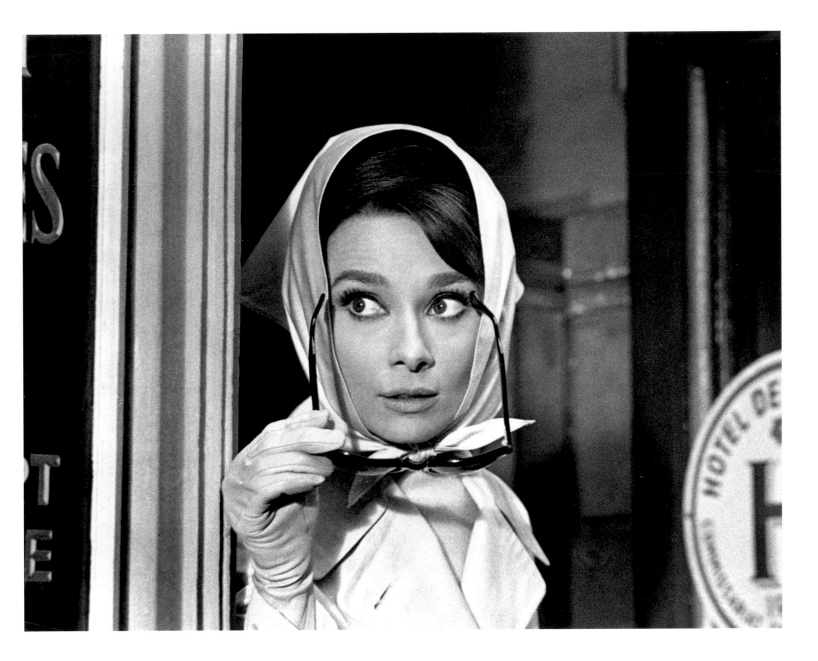

'Charade' made French tailored costumes and pillbox hats the height of fashion, and even the old-fashioned headscarf recovered its popularity. The big sunglasses had been a must ever since 'Tiffany's'.

91

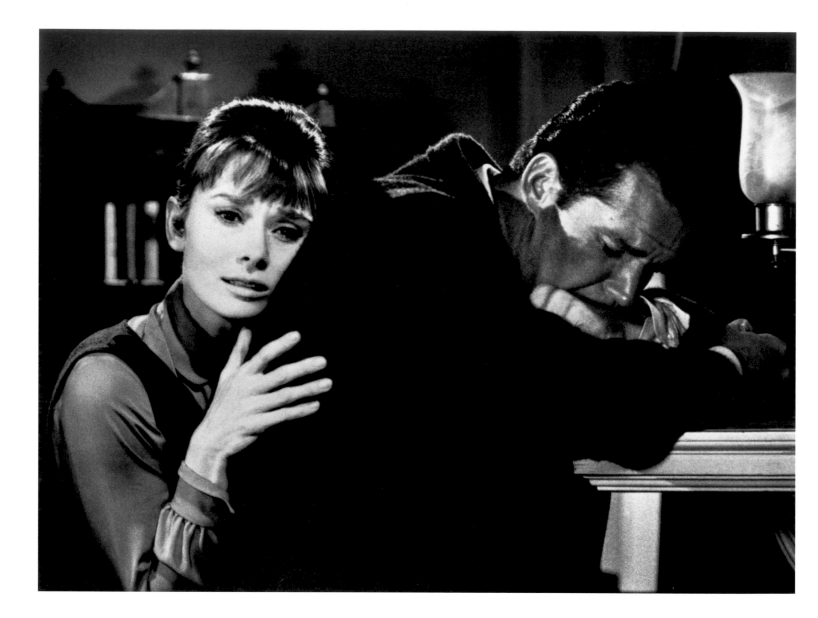

A serious part and a delicate subject: Audrey Hepburn as a slandered teacher in William Wyler's 'The Children's Hour', with her co-star James Garner. Publicity still by Bob Willoughby, 1961.

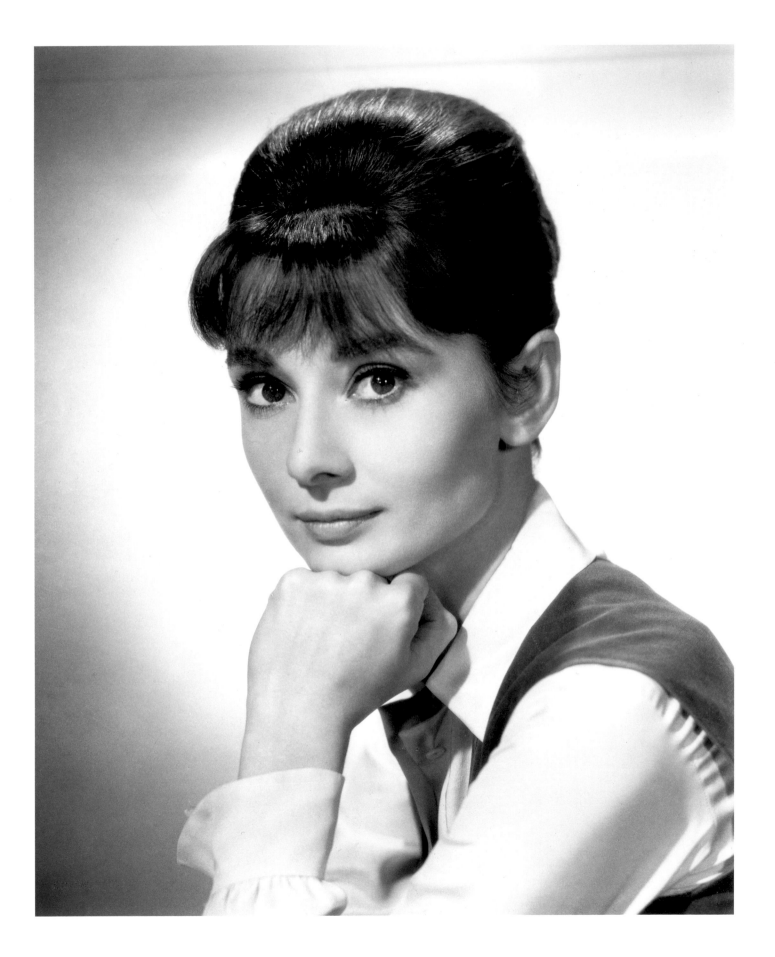

Publicity portrait for 'The Children's Hour', 1961. 93

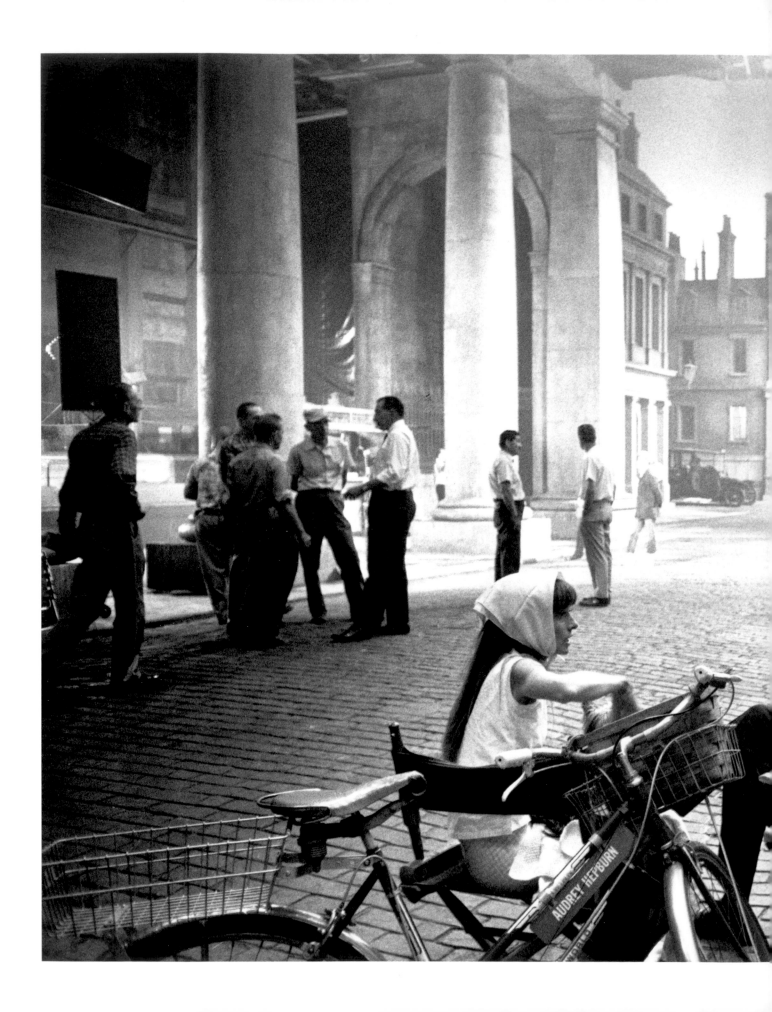

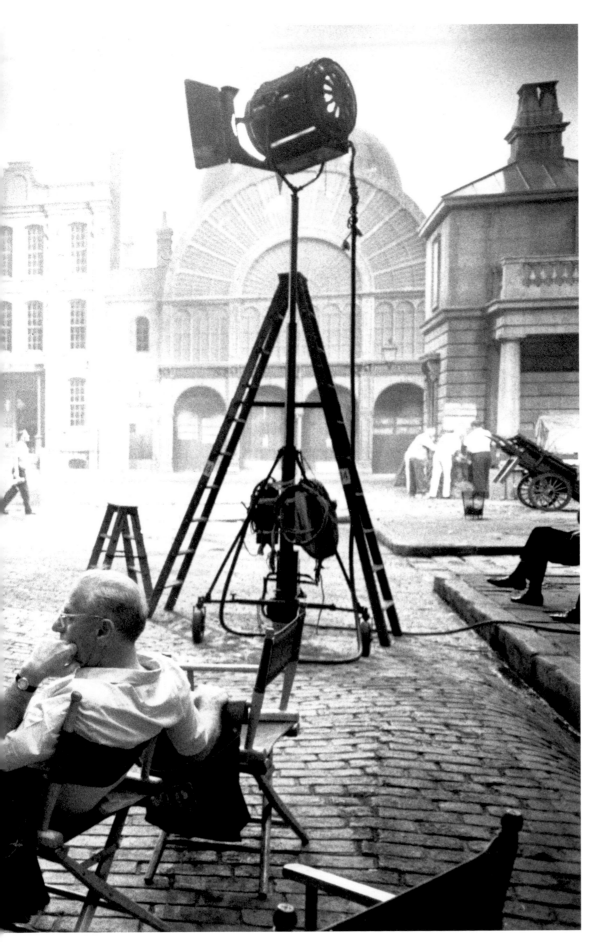

On the set of 'My Fair Lady':
Audrey Hepburn with director
George Cukor. In the film version,
costing millions, of the Broadway
hit musical, there was little trace
of George Bernard Shaw's original
'Pygmalion'.
Photo by Bob Willoughby, 1963.

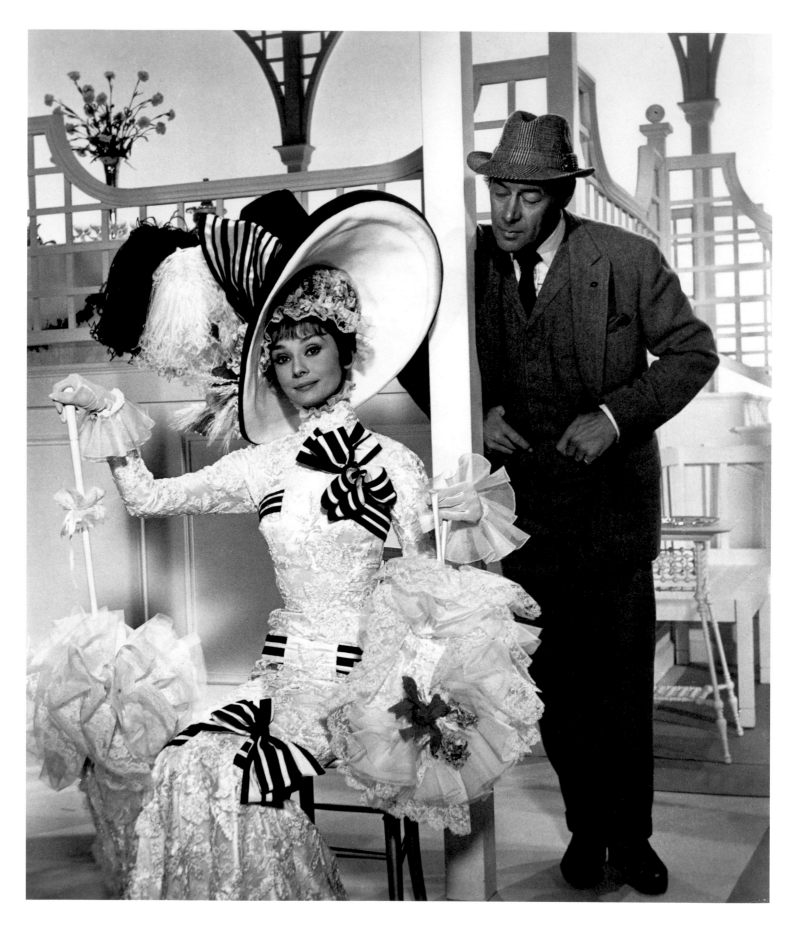

Professor Higgins (Rex Harrison) examines the result of his efforts: Eliza Doolittle, the flower-girl, has become a perfect lady.

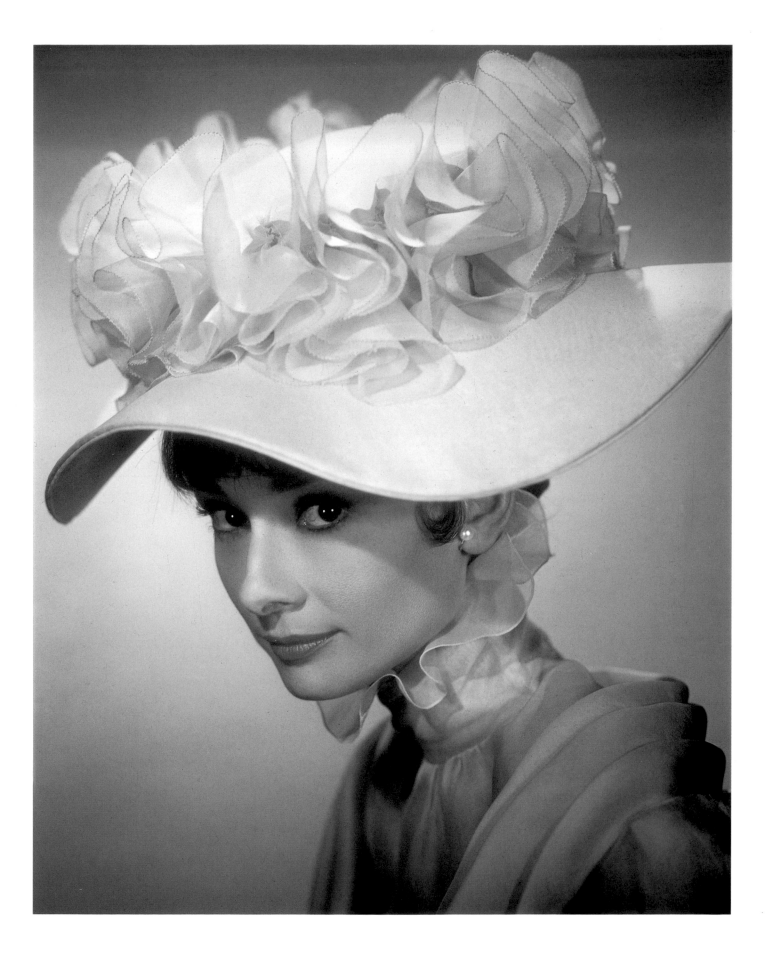

Publicity portrait for 'My Fair Lady'.

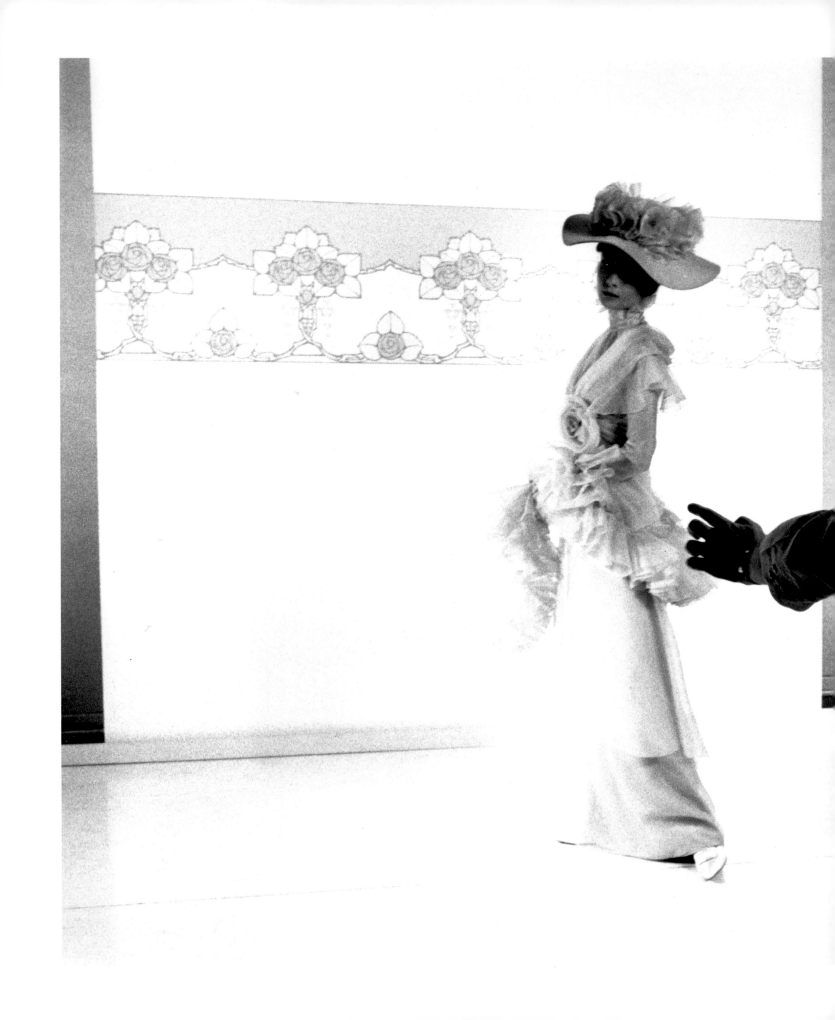

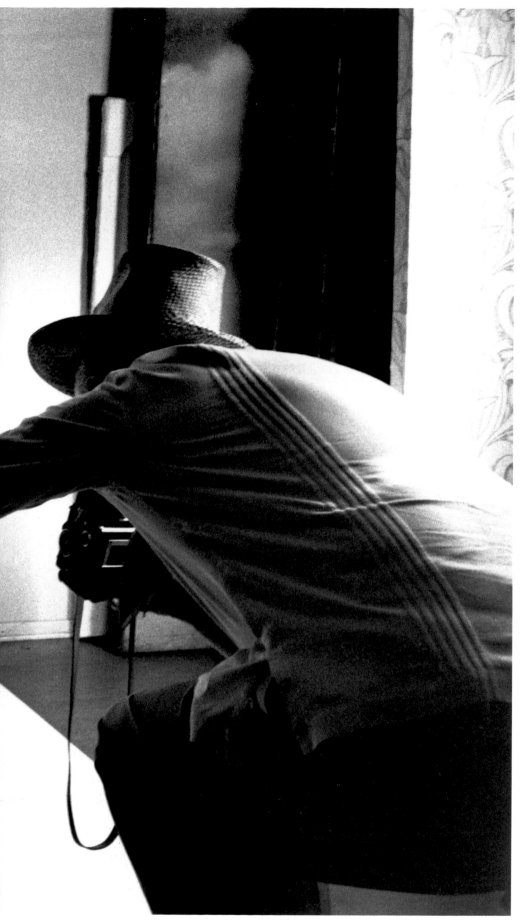

For 'My Fair Lady', Cecil Beaton not only
took photographs, as seen here; he was also
responsible for the expensive costumes and the
no less opulent décor and furnishings.
Photo by Bob Willoughby, 1963.

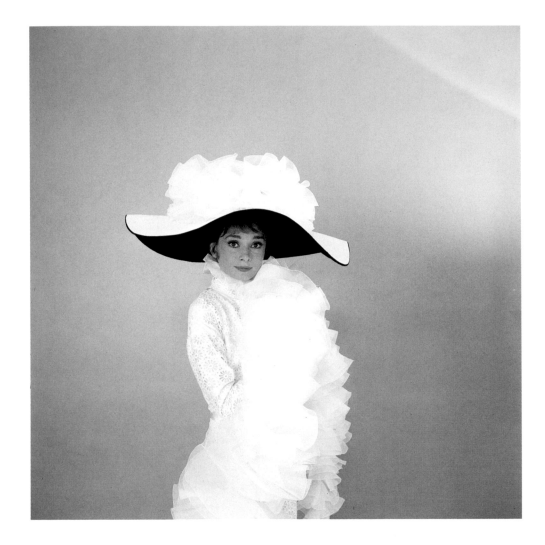

'Lady Eliza', all in white and as beautiful as a nineteenth-century portrait. Photo by Cecil Beaton.

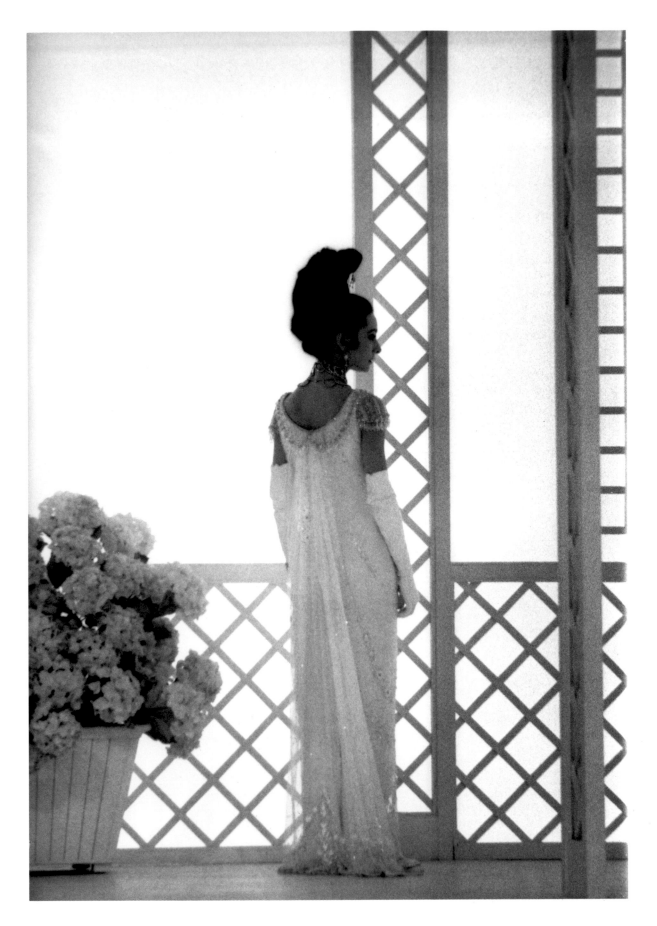

The former flower-girl in evening dress, standing beside a luxuriant bouquet.
Publicity still for 'My Fair Lady' by Bob Willoughby.

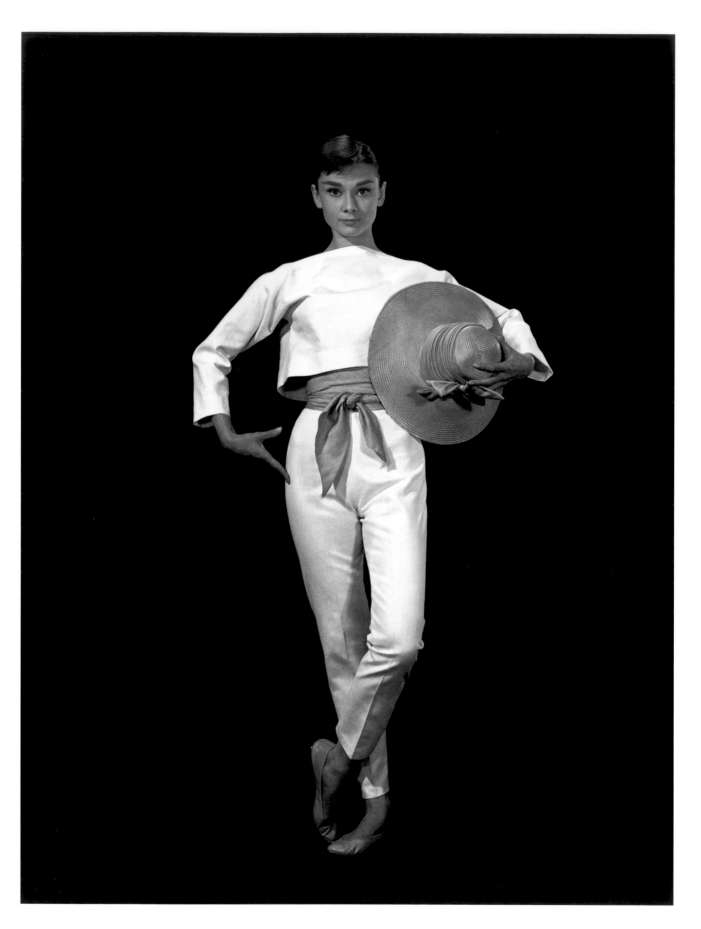

*The much-copied 'Hepburn look', here in the sports / tomboy version, with narrow trousers, flat shoes,
and bobbed hair . . .*

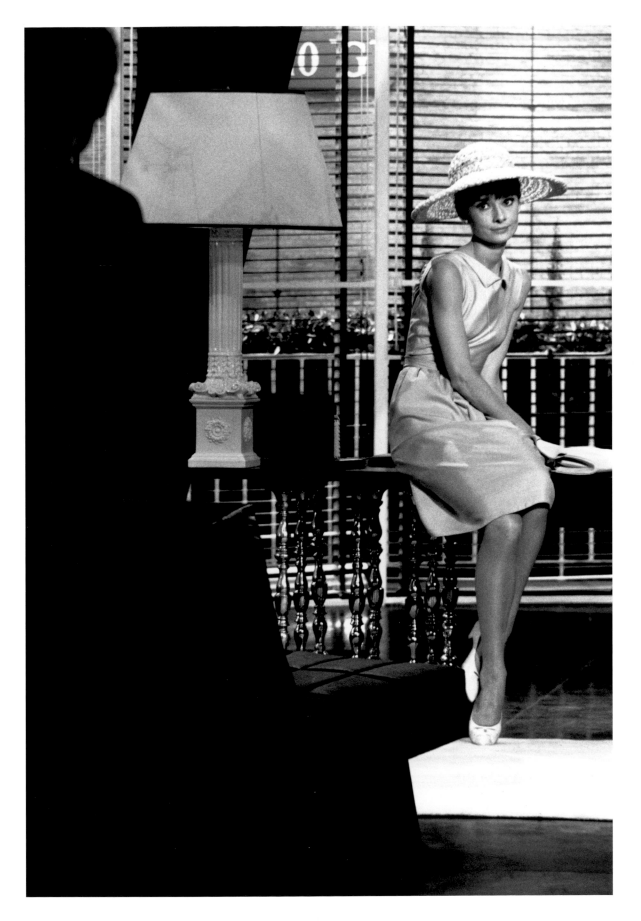

... and here elegantly feminine in a projecting hat and afternoon dress by Givenchy. Film still by Bob Willoughby from 'Paris When It Sizzles', 1963.

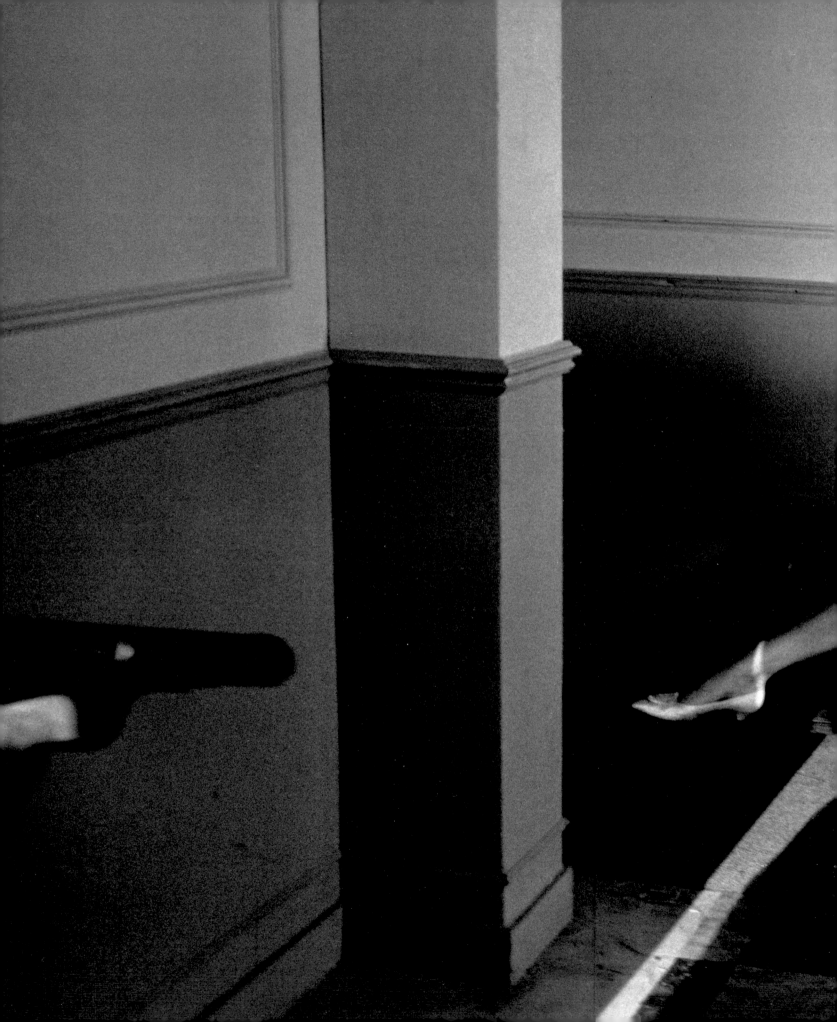

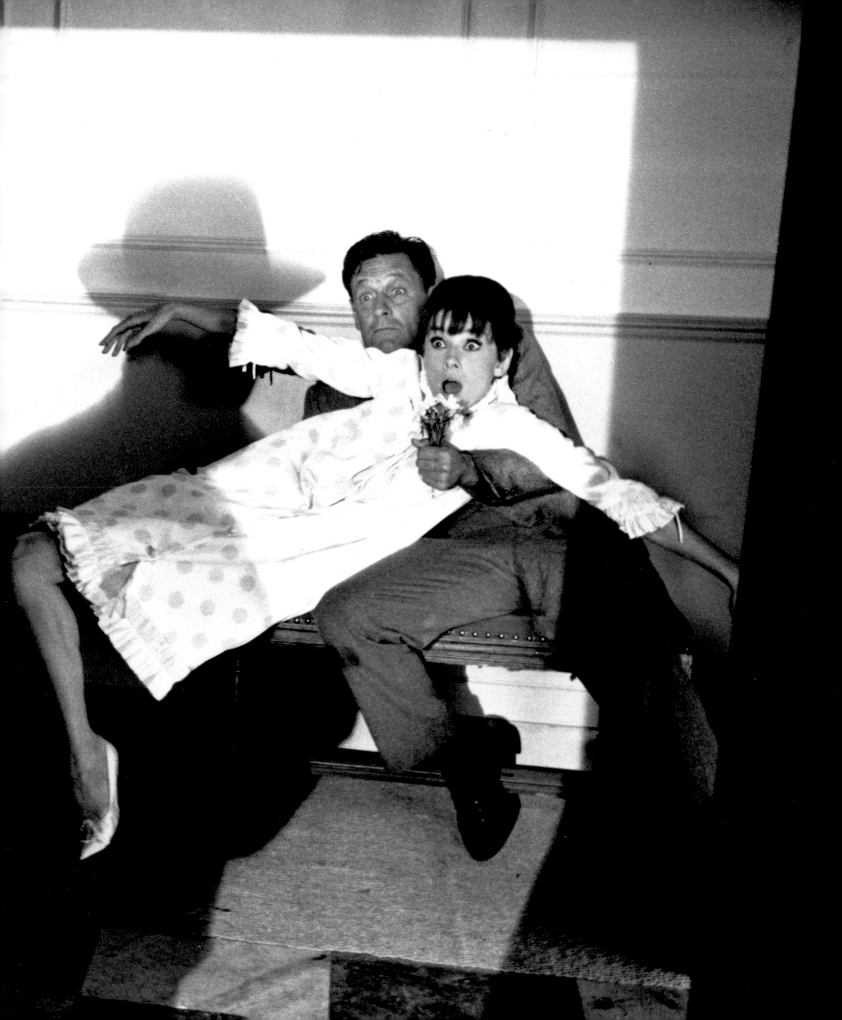

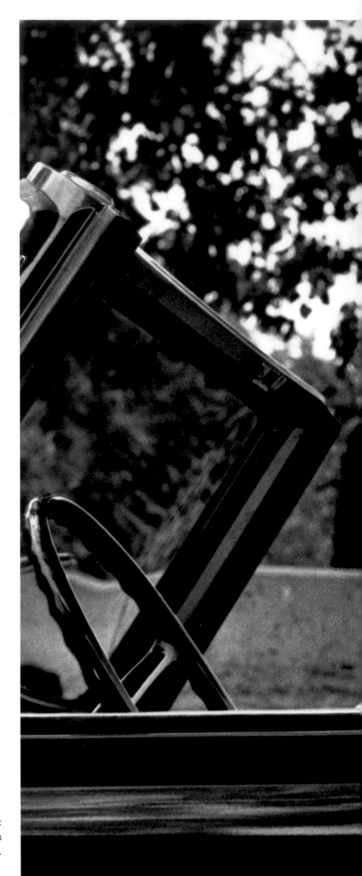

Preceding two pages:
A tricky situation: Audrey Hepburn with her co-star William Holden
in 'Paris When It Sizzles'. Photo by Bob Willoughby.

Dressed in Givenchy's 1965 collection, Audrey Hepburn
gets mixed up in some funny business as the daughter of an art forger
in 'How to Steal a Million'.

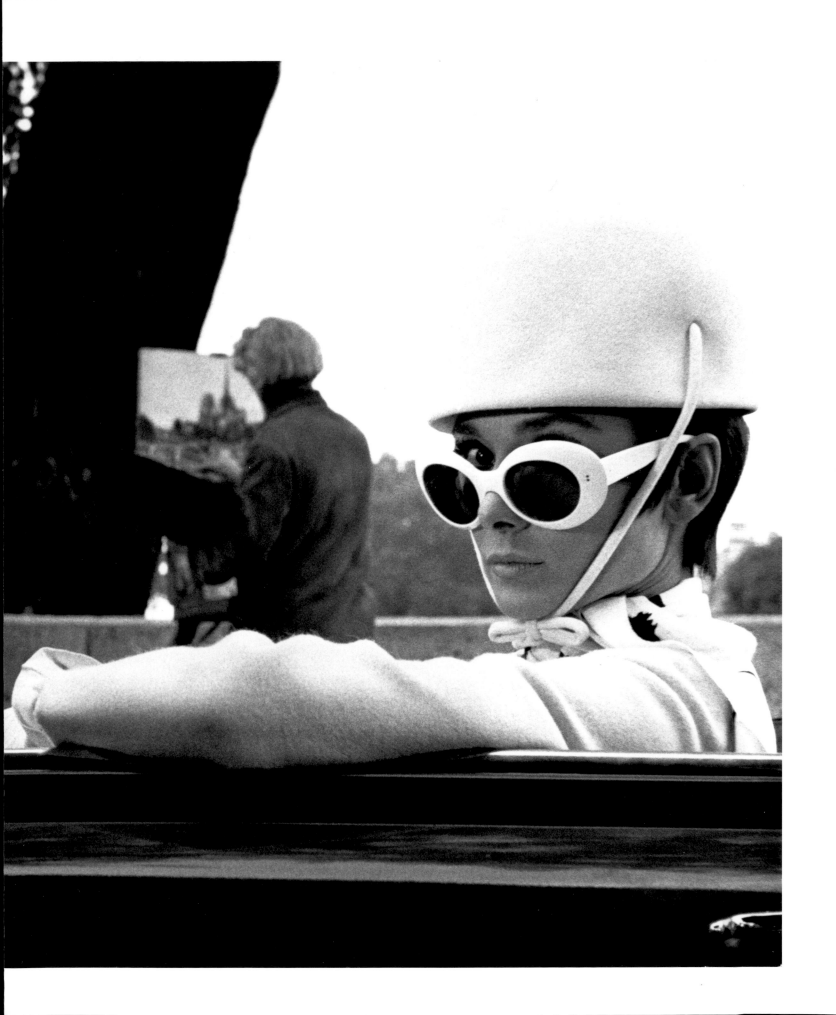

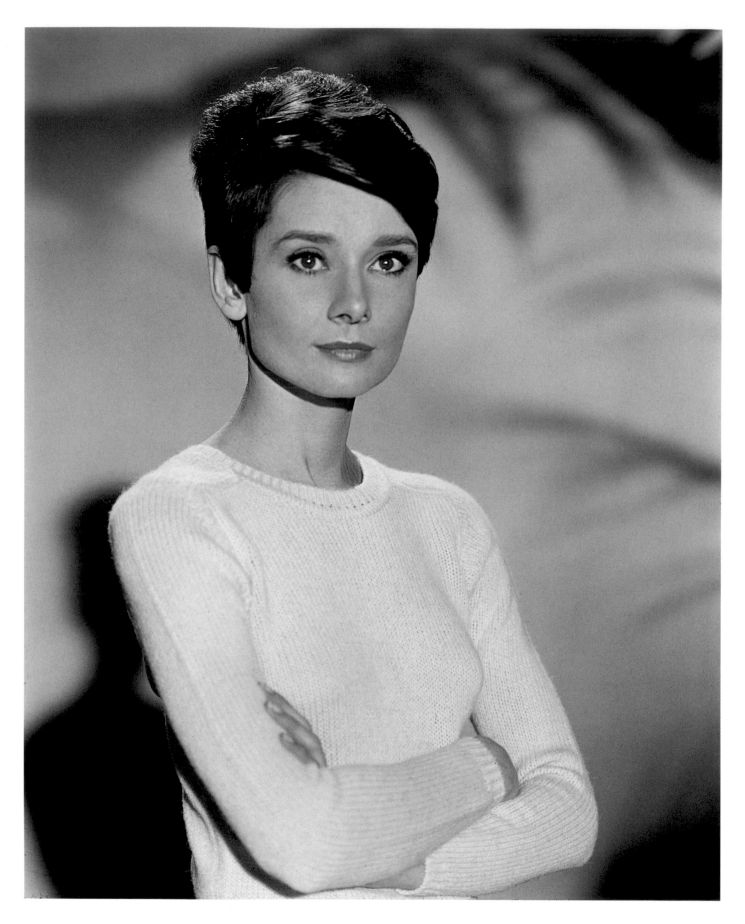

In 'Wait Until Dark' in 1966/67, Audrey Hepburn plays a young blind woman being chased by a psychopathic gangster. She prepared herself for the difficult part by attending a school for the blind.

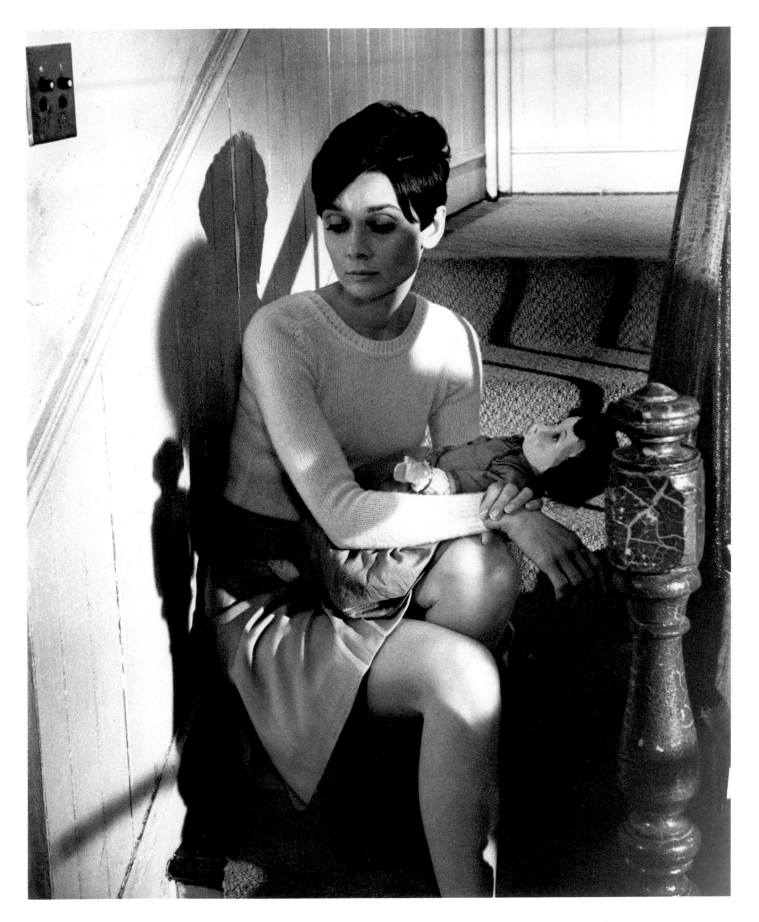

Film still from 'Wait Until Dark', with her arms round the doll in which the sought-after heroin has been concealed.

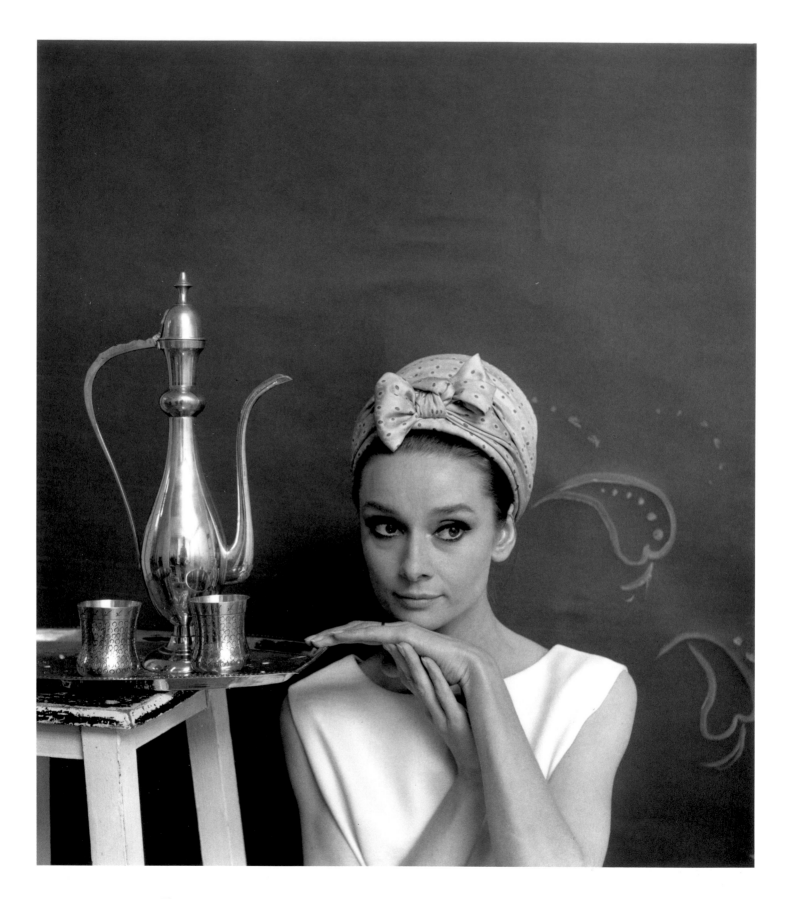

These two portrait studies are by Cecil Beaton, and show a more serious, almost melancholy, side of Audrey Hepburn. The photo on the right, in particular, recalls contemporary Beaton portraits of Maria Callas. Isabella Rossellini's advertising image was also modelled on this portrait.

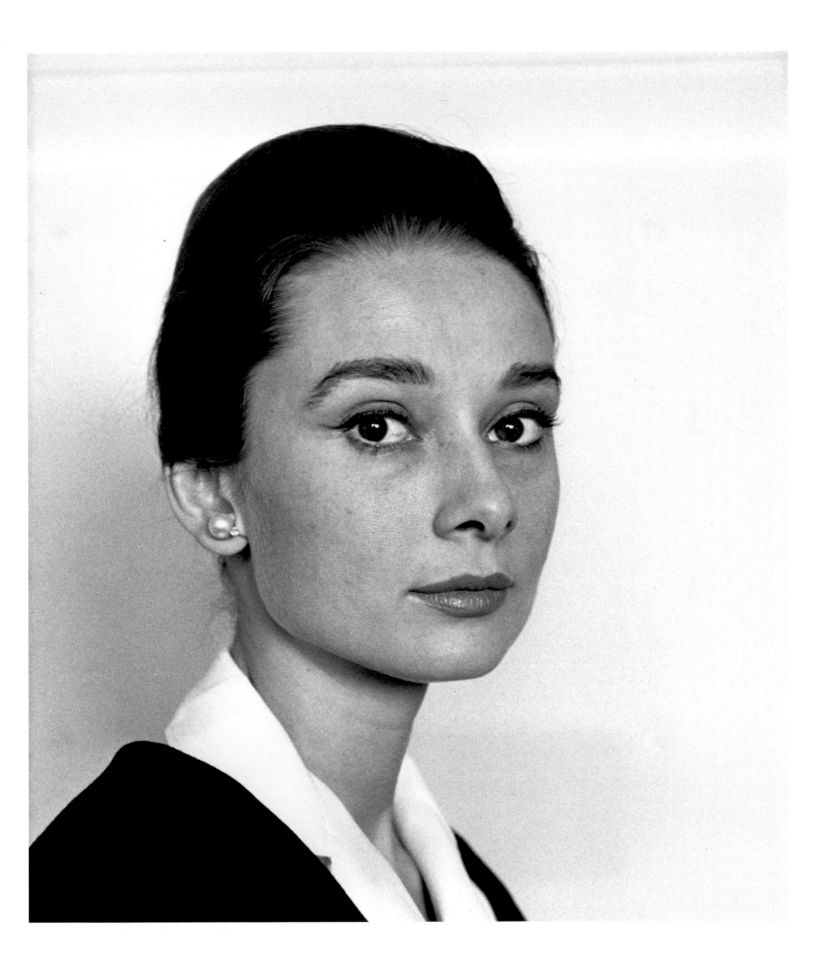

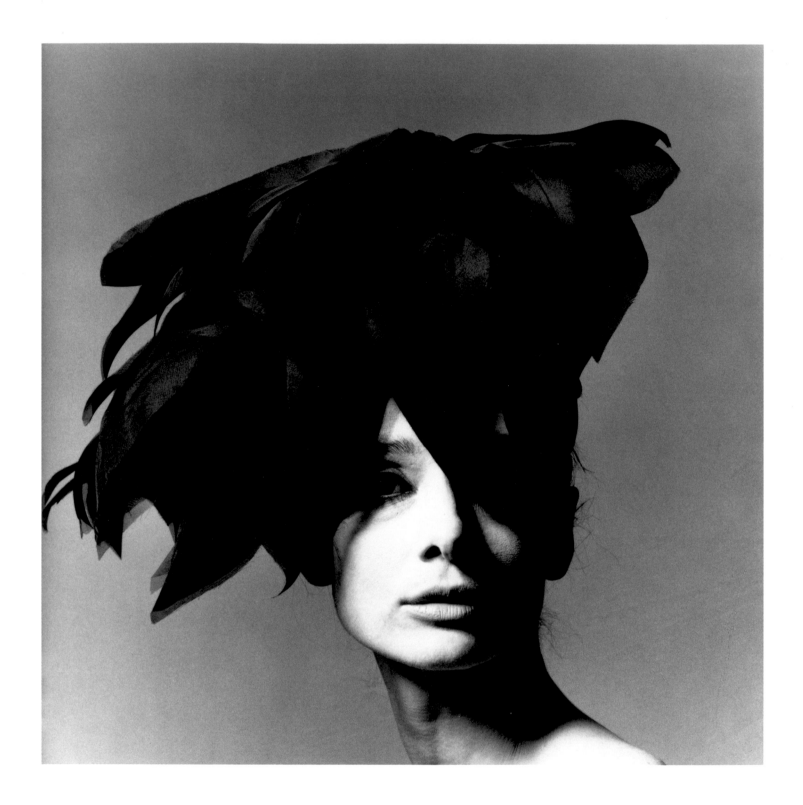

Bert Stern, a famous representative of the younger generation of photographers,
produced a much more avant-garde Audrey Hepburn. Above: a dramatically lit portrait with a hat;
right: a fashion shot with Mel Ferrer.

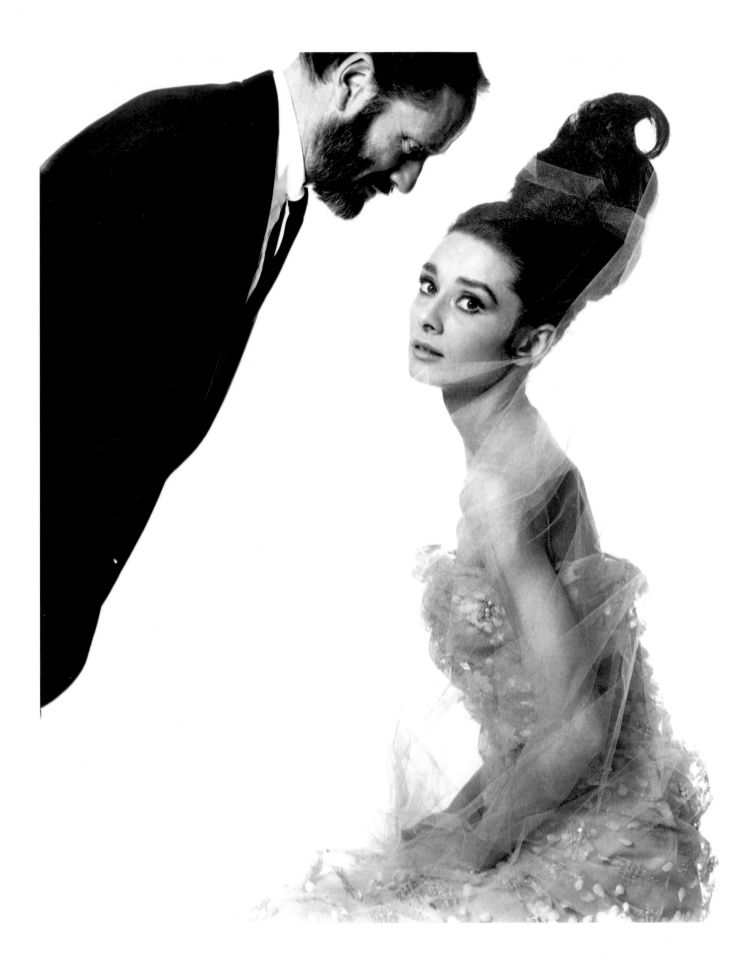

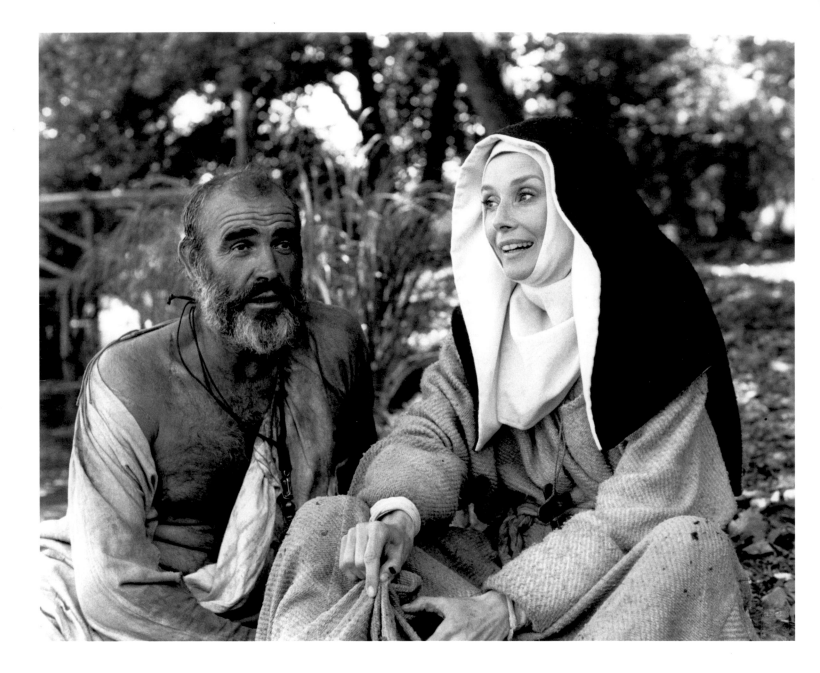

Her comeback after a break lasting nearly ten years. Sean Connery and Audrey Hepburn play the
ageing Robin Hood and Maid Marian. The film came out in 1976.

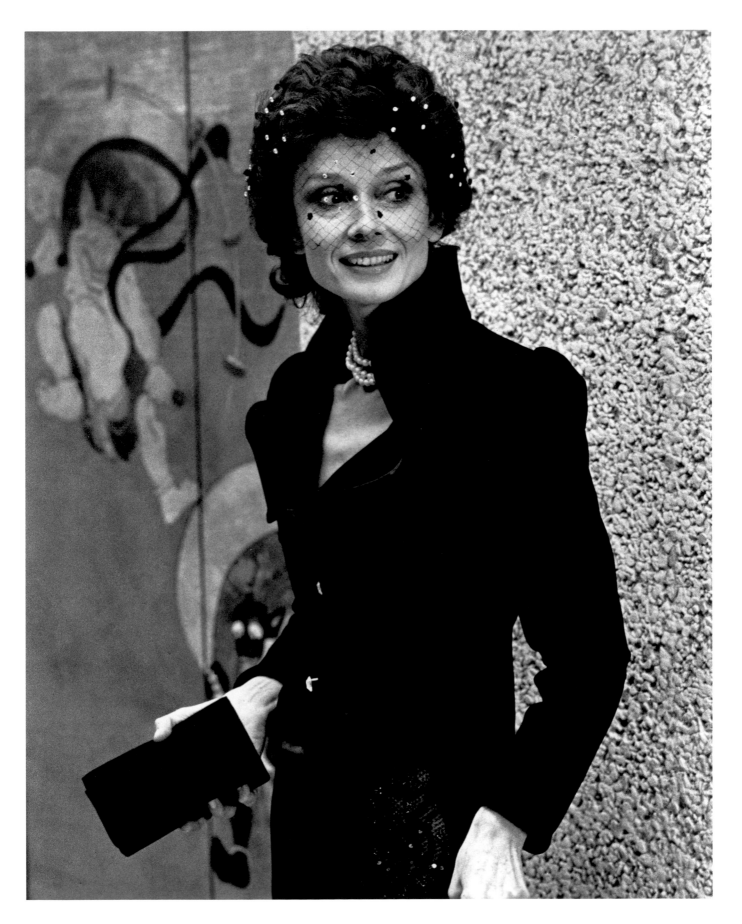

One of Audrey Hepburn's last major film roles was as a rich heiress being hunted down by killers in
the high-society thriller 'Bloodline', 1979.

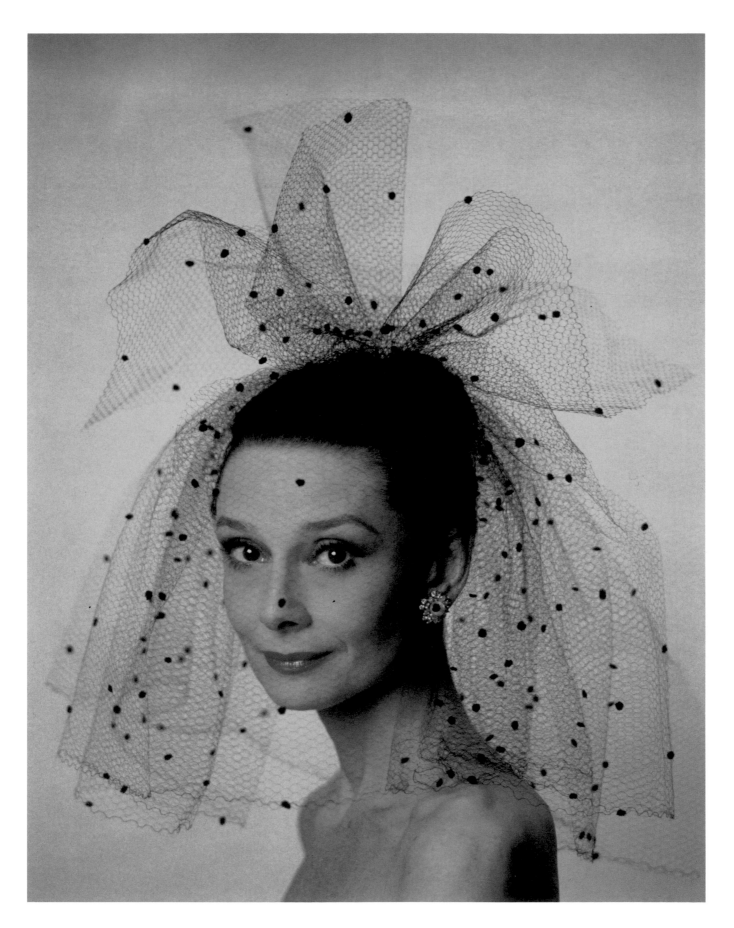

Publicity portrait for 'Bloodline'. Audrey Hepburn, here attractively veiled, celebrated her fiftieth birthday in 1979, the year this photo was taken.

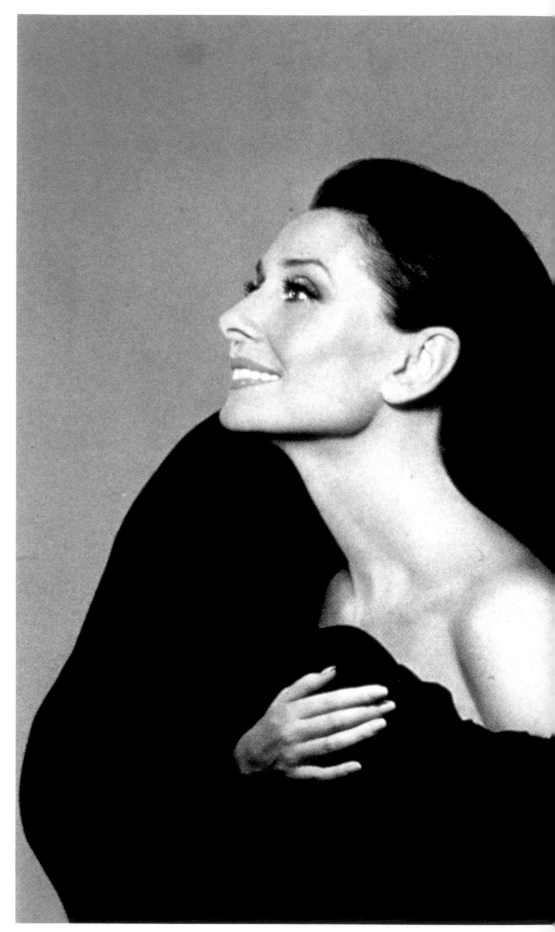

Radiant and spotless. A pair of Audrey Hepburns for a Revlon advertising campaign, photographed by Richard Avedon.

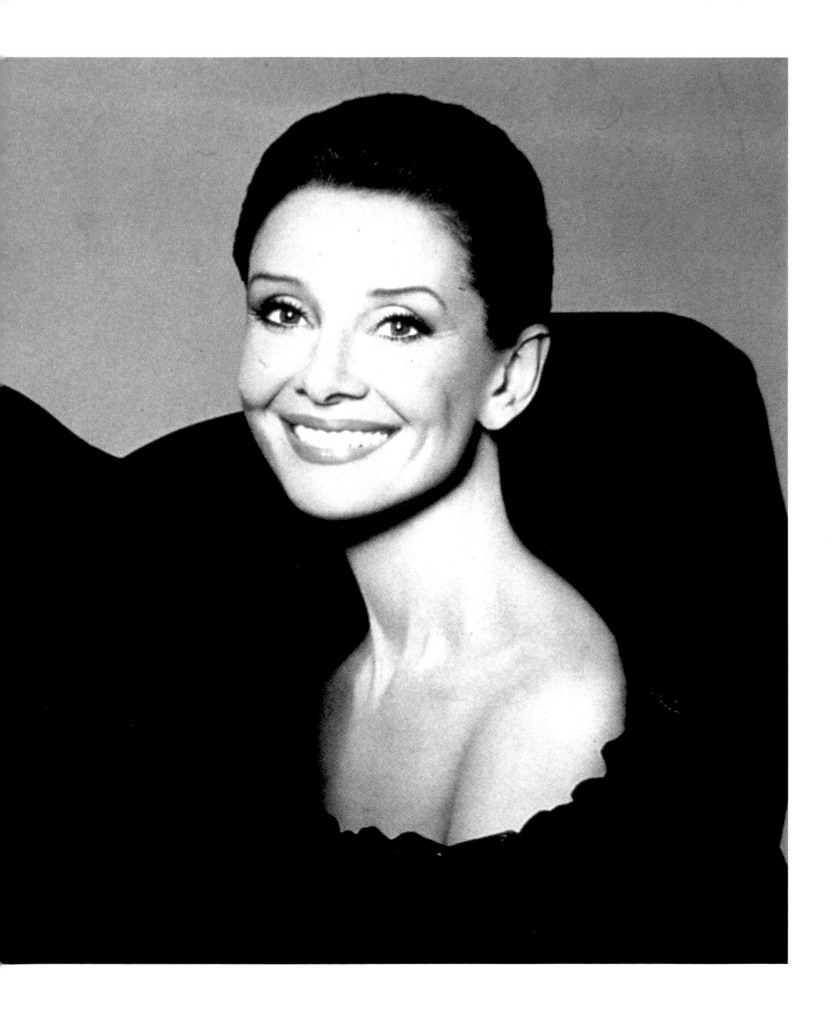

In March 1983, Audrey Hepburn visits a gala performance by the Ballet Rambert in London.
Thirty-five years before, she had studied classical ballet at the famous Rambert School.
Photo by David Gaywood.

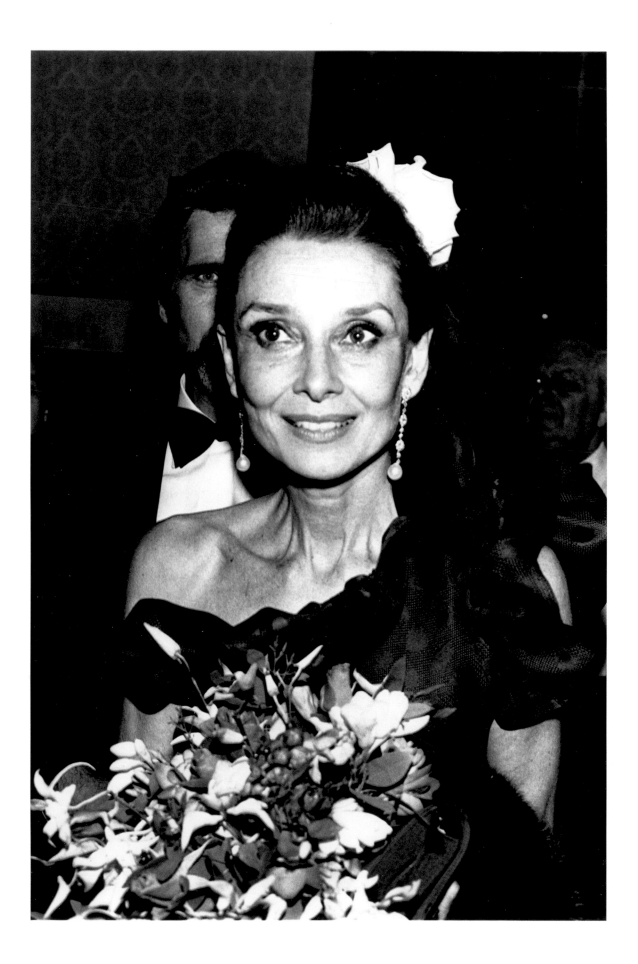

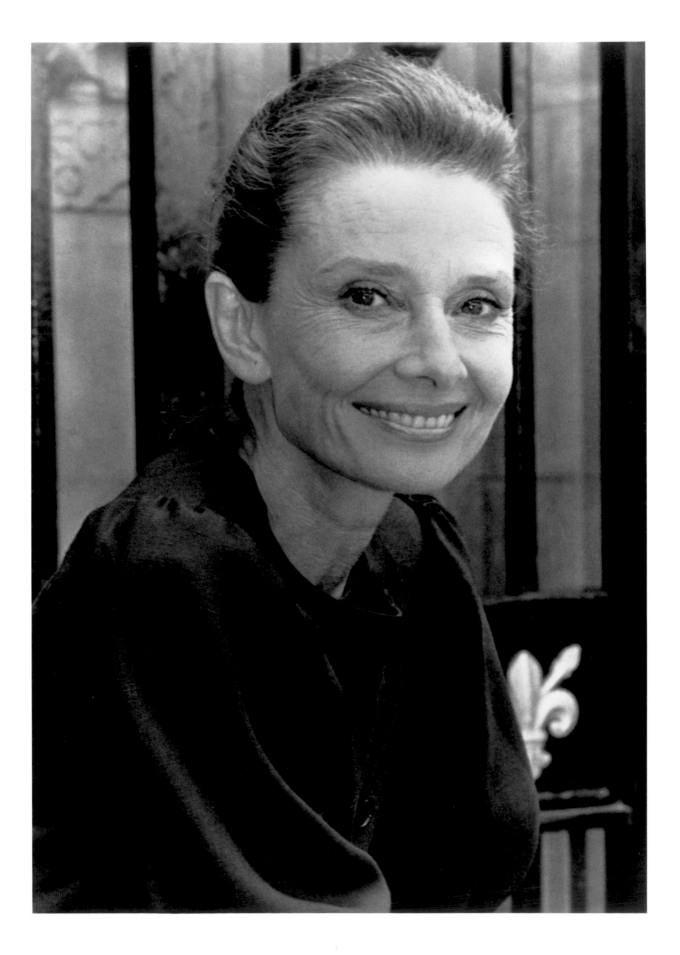

The year of her sixtieth birthday, 1989.

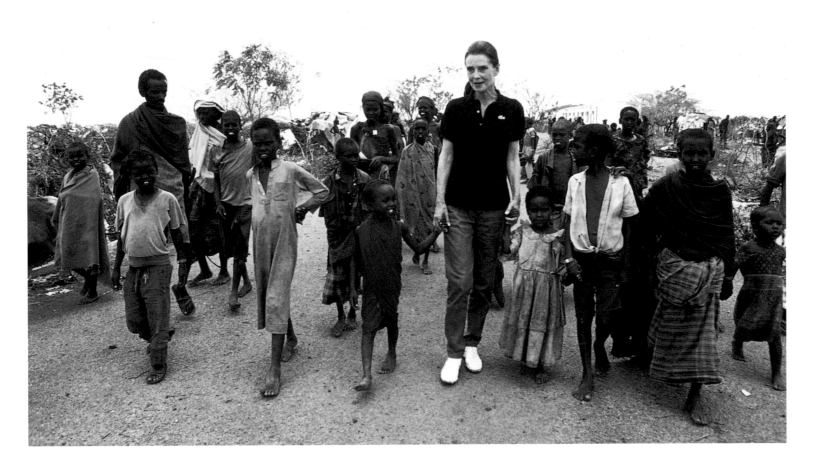

Audrey Hepburn devotes herself to her new duties as a special emissary for UNICEF. In September 1992,
she travels through the areas struck by famine in Somalia.

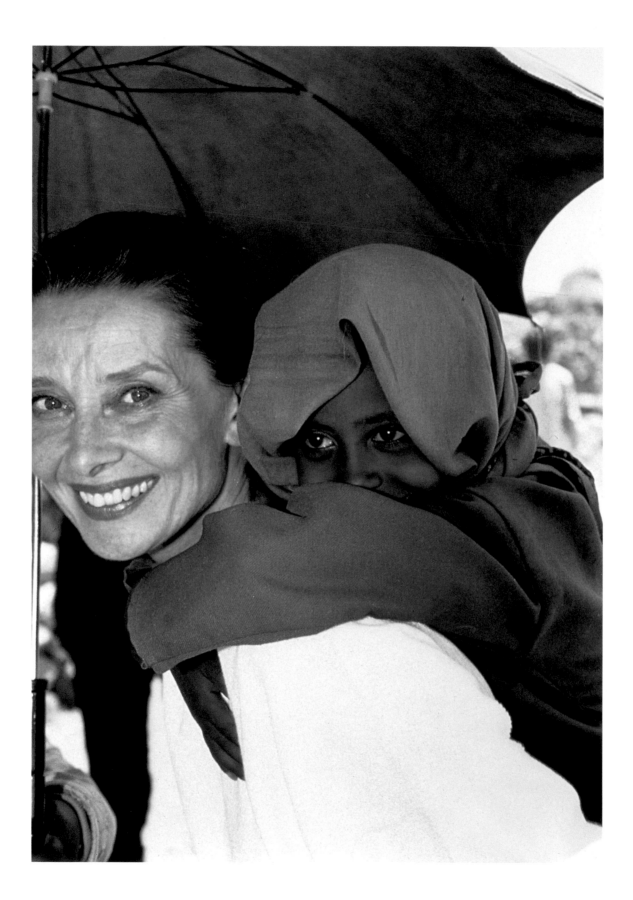

A familiar image: in 1959, as Sister Lukas in 'The Nun's Story', she looked after children in the Belgian Congo. In 1989, in real life, she is seen comforting starving children in Ethiopia.

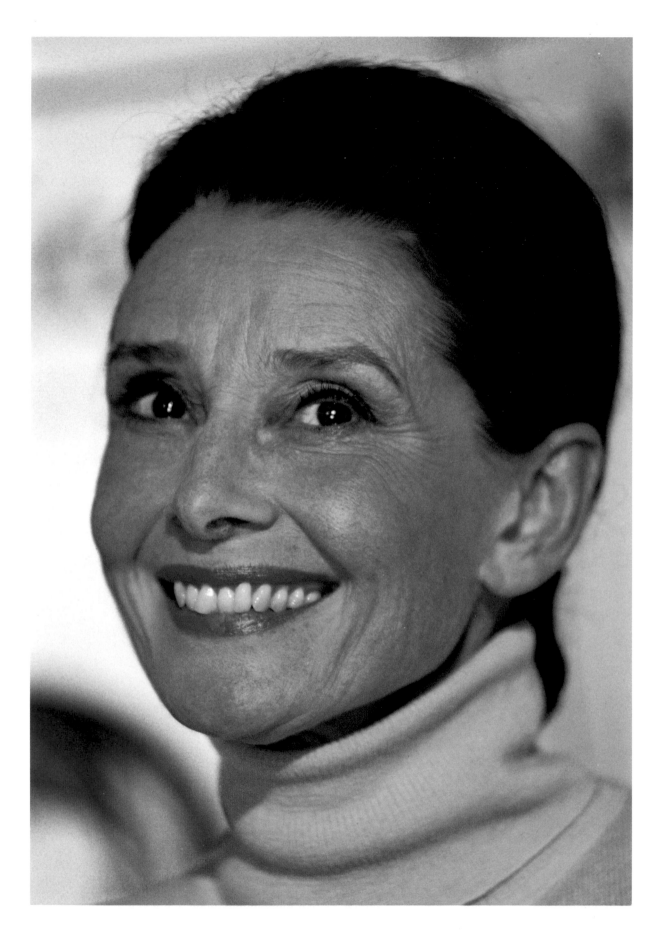

One of the last portraits, taken by Simon Walker in September 1992.
Audrey Hepburn died in January 1993.

Biography

1929 Audrey Hepburn (Edda Kathleen van Heemstra Hepburn-Ruston) is born on 4 May in Brussels. Her mother, Ella van Heemstra, a Dutch baroness, had married an Irish banker, John Victor Anthony Hepburn-Ruston, as her second husband; she already had two sons by her first marriage.

As a child, Edda / Audrey refuses to play with dolls, preferring instead to read Kipling stories and Edgar Wallace. From a very early age, she is attracted to music and dancing. She takes ballet lessons. She goes to school in England during the winter, spending her summers on the Heemstra family's country estate near Arnhem.

1935 Her father leaves the family.

1938 Her parents are divorced. Edda is sent to a boarding school in England.

1939–45 She spends the war in Arnhem. She attends the city's conservatory and dreams of a career as a prima ballerina. However, the prospect recedes further and further away after the German occupation in 1940 and the destruction in 1944 of both the family's country home and of the Arnhem Conservatory.

1945 The family moves to Amsterdam. Edda takes lessons from Sonia Gaskell, then Holland's most respected ballet teacher, but the school soon has to be closed down. At Sonia Gaskell's, Edda is 'discovered' by Charles Huguenot, a Durch documentary film-maker, and he hires her to take part in an advertising film, *Nederlands in 7 Lessen*; she plays the part of a KLM air hostess.

1948 Edda persuades her mother that the two of them should move to London, and immediately begins to call herself Audrey Hepburn. She has been awarded a — fairly modest — grant to attend Marie Rambert's famous ballet school, where Nijinsky and others studied.

Both mother and daughter earn their living doing caretaking work and temporary jobs; Audrey gives French lessons, and does modelling, tall and slim as she is, for advertising photos.

Audrey is chosen from among 3000 applicants as one of ten chorus girls for the London production of the Broadway musical *High Button Shoes*. The show is premièred on 22 December, and 291 performances follow.

1949 The theatrical impresario Cecil Landeau notices 'the third chorus girl from the left'; he hires Audrey for his new musical, *Sauce Tartare*, which is premièred in May, goes through 433 performances, and is the hit of the season.

1950 In Landeau's following show, *Sauce Piquante*, Audrey is allowed to take part in a few of the sketches. She takes acting lessons.

1951 Associated British Films, specializing in comedies, notice Audrey Hepburn. Mario Zampi, director of *Laughter in Paradise*, offers her the leading role in the film. Owing to commitments with Landeau, Audrey has to decline the offer, but she does receive a minor part. After her short appearance as a girl with a vendor's tray, she is nevertheless rewarded with a seven-year contract with Associated British Films.

After the shooting of *Young Wives' Tales*, a situation comedy, she meets James Hanson, the son of a wealthy haulage contractor; the romance between them continues for several years.

A few of the scenes for the harmless slapstick musical *Nous irons à Monte Carlo*, in which her appearance lasts all of twelve minutes, are shot on the Italian Riviera. In Monte Carlo's Hôtel de Paris, an older lady in a wheelchair can be seen watching Audrey during the shooting, and Colette is immediately convinced that 'she is my Gigi'. The Broadway production of Colette's comedy of manners *Gigi*, which is premièred on 24 November, is a resounding success. A new star is born: Audrey Hepburn.

1952 Even while rehearsals for *Gigi* are still going on, Paramount is negotiating to acquire Colette's discovery. For his film *Roman Holiday*, William Wyler still needs a princess to play opposite the photojournalist Gregory Peck. She passes her camera test with flying colours. Audrey Hepburn breaks off her engagement with James Hanson and, during Broadway's summer break, flies to Rome to shoot her first Hollywood film and worldwide hit.

A new character type is born: the fragile, but self-aware child / woman with big, intelligent eyes, with a good family background, refreshingly natural and, in spite of all her aristocratic composure, touchingly in need of protection. Audrey Hepburn becomes a screen idol overnight. She embodies the ideals of millions of teenagers all over the world, and is enthusiastically welcomed as an alternative to the sex-bombs and pin-ups of the 'clean' 1950s.

1953 *Sabrina*, directed by Billy Wilder and produced once again by Paramount, reinforces her still fresh image. The partner of Humphrey Bogart and William Holden, Sabrina, an unprepossessing chauffeur's daughter, blossoms like Cinderella into an attractive beauty full of Paris chic. Audrey Hepburn chooses Hubert de Givenchy to supply her wardrobe following this transformation, and she remains his loyal customer for the rest of her life. The fashion image of the new star is therefore also clearly set — and with it the style of the whole 1950s.

Prizes and awards accumulate: *Life* makes her 'Woman of the Year', she wins the New York Film Critics' Prize, and the British magazine *Picturegoer*'s gold medal, and ultimately an Oscar nomination as Best Actress for *Sabrina*. At the London première of *Roman Holiday*, she meets Mel Ferrer. They start making joint plans for theatrical work.

1954 Jean Giraudoux's mythic and romantic fable, *Undine*,

is the perfect vehicle for their joint appearance on the Broadway stage. The production, featuring Audrey as the water-nymph and Mel Ferrer as the lovesick knight, opens on 18 February to standing ovations, and earns Audrey a Tony Award as the best female actress.

In March, she receives her first and only Oscar for her performance in *Roman Holiday*.

In September, Audrey Hepburn and Mel Ferrer marry in Switzerland.

1955 Audrey declines any film projects that might separate her from her husband for longer periods. When the Italian producer Dino de Laurentiis offers her and Mel Ferrer leading parts in a wide-screen production of Tolstoy's *War and Peace*, she agrees. Audrey becomes pregnant, and suffers a miscarriage; the role of Natasha does not really suit her, and also is not really in keeping with her screen image, as the critics are not slow to point out. Apart from that, the spectacular crowd scenes and battles appear to be much more important to the producer than Tolstoy's three main characters. The film's success does not meet expectations.

1956 With *Funny Face*, an MGM remake of the 1927 musical, Audrey returns to her successful role as a modern Cinderella. Fred Astaire plays the 'prince', in this case a fashion photographer. Richard Avedon is responsible for visual design.

At the end of the year, she plays Ariane opposite Gary Cooper in *Love in the Afternoon*, once again directed by Billy Wilder.

1957 A change of image begins: with *A Nun's Story*, directed by Fred Zinnemann, Audrey moves towards more serious material. Her acting achievement, and the film's success — she is nominated for an Oscar for the third time — give her career a new direction: she finally, and successfully, moves away from being just a 'funny face' in romantic Cinderella parts.

1959 She plays her first part in a western, as the Kiowa girl Rachel in John Huston's *The Unforgiven*, for a fee of

$ 200,000. During shooting, Audrey, who is once again pregnant, falls off a horse. Four months later, her second miscarriage occurs, and she has to decline an offer from Alfred Hitchcock.

1960 Her son Sean is born on 17 July.

In September, the shooting of Truman Capote's *Breakfast at Tiffany's* begins in New York.

1961 The (watered-down) film version of Capote's vicious social satire reaches the cinemas in America in November and is a big hit, even though the part of the happy-go-lucky callgirl, Holly Golightly, does not seem tailor-made for Audrey. The child/woman had grown up and had replaced the unvanquished, naïve self-confidence of her early heroines with a psychologically subtle interpretation of her own character type. Both the public and the critics were delighted, and Hollywood's reaction was a fourth Oscar nomination.

In the same year, she makes *The Children's Hour*, another excursion into serious character acting, which only met with moderate acclaim.

1962 Her new image is successfully exploited in Stanley Donen's *Charade*. In a plot that has Hitchcock quality, and playing opposite Cary Grant, with whom she has an instinctive rapport, Audrey develops a talent for wit and tragicomedy that makes the film a box-office hit. The film conclusively turns Audrey into a much-imitated epitome of fashionable elegance. Once again, Givenchy designed her extensive wardrobe for the film.

The marriage between Hepburn and Ferrer begins to suffer from more and more serious crises.

1963 It is the year of *My Fair Lady*, the most spectacular and highly-paid role of Audrey's career. The film version of the highly successful Broadway musical based on Shaw's play *Pygmalion*, directed by George Cukor, turns into an orgy of décor and costumes costing a total of $17 million. Cecil Beaton is responsible for the opulent décor and the costumes, which alone eat up a million dollars. The shooting of the film is prolonged and tension-laden. To her considerable disappointment, Audrey is not allowed to sing the songs herself; the press never stops comparing her with Julie Andrews, who played Eliza Doolittle in the Broadway version. Her continuing private troubles make her irritable and unusually disagreeable.

1964 *My Fair Lady* brings in $33 million in America alone, and saves Warner Bros. from threatened bankruptcy. The production is awarded seven Oscars, including one for Best Film, and one for Rex Harrison as Best Actor. Audrey receives nothing; the critics celebrate her as an ideal lady, but claim she lacks credibility as the slovenly flower-girl Eliza.

1965 Two productions made within the space of a short time — *How to Steal a Million* with Peter O'Toole as co-star, and *Two for the Road* with Albert Finney, the story of a married couple — take advantage of Audrey's continuing fame following *Tiffany* and *Charade*. Her maturing screen image is gradually allowing the upper-class girl to grow into a modern woman, even one who can commit adultery.

A third miscarriage temporarily smooths over Hepburn's and Ferrer's marriage difficulties.

1967 Audrey is now one of the actresses most in demand throughout the world, and can command fees of over a million dollars. Mel Ferrer's career, by contrast, has reached its nadir, and even their last joint effort proves incapable of restoring it. The thriller *Wait Until Dark*, directed by Ferrer, in which Audrey takes the lead part as Susie Hendrix, a blind girl, is a box-office success and brings Audrey her fifth Oscar nomination; but it fails to save their marriage. In the autumn, after her fourth miscarriage, Audrey announces her separation from Mel Ferrer.

1968–69 During a cruise, Audrey meets the psychiatrist Andrea Dotti, from Rome; he is considerably younger than her. After the difficult process of getting her divorce, the couple are married in January 1969 and move to Rome.

1970 Audrey's second son, Luca, is born.

1970–75 During the following five years, she consistently declines all film offers, including one from Luchino Visconti, who hopes to have her in his film *Gruppo di famiglia in un interno* (1974), on the grounds that she needs time to bring up her two sons. On the other hand, she is only too well aware that there are no adequate parts left for her. The classic Hollywood to which she owes her career, and in the shaping of which she herself had had a decisive role, has ceased to exist. A new generation of film-makers has no use for her character type, that relic from a past that needs to be superseded.

1976 Her marriage with Andrea Dotti turns out to be fraught with difficulties and disappointments. This is one of the reasons why, after ten years, Audrey takes the risk of attempting a comeback. Directed by Richard Lester, she plays Maid Marian, the ageing companion of an equally aged Robin Hood (Sean Connery).

1978 As a favour to her friend Terence Young, Audrey accepts the part of an industrial heiress in an unconvincing thriller about rich people, *Bloodline*.

1980 During the summer, Audrey separates from Andrea Dotti.

The third film after her comeback, Peter Bogdanovich's *They All Laughed*, is not a great success either. Audrey decides to withdraw from the film business permanently.

1981 Audrey finds a new male companion, the Dutch-born actor Robert Wolders, widower of the Hollywood star Merle Oberon.

1982–87 The divorce between Hepburn and Dotti becomes official in 1982. During the following years, Audrey travels widely, and looks after her growing sons. She strictly declines all film proposals, even a highly lucrative one from Warner, a part in the TV series *The Thornbirds*. Finally, she makes one exception: in the TV production *Love Among Thieves*, she plays an elegant concert pinanist, dressed by Givenchy, who gets mixed up in all sorts of comical criminal adventures. The film is spurned by the critics as a superficial and distant echo of *Charade*.

1988 UNICEF, the United Nations Children's Fund, appoints Audrey as a special emissary. In the years that follow, she devotes herself completely to the work of UNICEF. She travels to Latin America and Africa, organizes appeals for donations, makes speeches, and becomes patron of various organizations.

1989 Audrey faces the camera for the last time. As a white-robed, ethereal guardian angel in Steven Spielberg's *Always*, she eases the path of a crashed pilot into the hereafter.

1993 Audrey Hepburn dies of cancer on 20 January.

Filmography

LONDON

1. NEDERLANDS IN 7 LESSEN
   Netherlands 1948, b/w, producer H. M. Josephson
   Director: Charles Huguenot van der Linden

2. LAUGHTER IN PARADISE
   England 1951, b/w, Associated British / Pathé
   Director: Mario Zampi

3. ONE WILD OAT
   England 1951, b/w, Eros-Coronet
   Director: Charles Saunders

4. YOUNG WIVES' TALES
   England 1951, b/w, Associated British / Allied Artists
   Director: Henry Cass

5. THE LAVENDER HILL MOB
   England 1951, b/w, Ealing / Rank / Universal
   Director: Charles Crichton; with Alec Guinness

6. THE SECRET PEOPLE
   England 1952, b/w, Ealing / Lippert
   Director: Thorold Dickinson; with Serge Reggiani

7. NOUS IRONS A MONTE CARLO
   France 1951, b/w, Hoche
   Director: Jean Boyer

   MONTE CARLO BABY
   English version 1952, b/w, Ventura / Filmmakers

HOLLYWOOD

8. ROMAN HOLIDAY
   USA 1953, b/w, Paramount
   Director: William Wyler; with Gregory Peck

9. SABRINA
   USA 1954, b/w, Paramount
   Director: Billy Wilder; with Humphrey Bogart and
   William Holden

10. WAR AND PEACE
    USA / Italy 1956, colour / VistaVision, Paramount
    Director: King Vidor; with Henry Fonda, Mel Ferrer,
    Vittorio Gassmann, and Anita Ekberg

11. FUNNY FACE
    USA 1957, colour / VistaVision, Paramount
    Director: Stanley Donen; with Fred Astaire

12. LOVE IN THE AFTERNOON
    USA 1957, b/w, Allied Artists
    Director: Billy Wilder; with Gary Cooper and
    Maurice Chevalier

13. GREEN MANSIONS
    USA 1959, colour / Cinemascope, MGM / Avon
    Director: Mel Ferrer; with Anthony Perkins

14. THE NUN'S STORY
    USA 1959, colour, Warner
    Director: Fred Zinnemann; with Peter Finch

15. THE UNFORGIVEN
    USA 1960, colour / Panavision, United Artists / James
    Productions / Hecht-Hill-Lancaster
    Director: John Huston; with Burt Lancaster

16. BREAKFAST AT TIFFANY'S
USA 1961, colour, Paramount
Director: Blake Edwards; with George Peppard

17. THE CHILDREN'S HOUR
USA 1961, b/w, United Artists / Mirisch Corporation
Director: William Wyler; with Shirley MacLaine
and James Garner

18. CHARADE
USA 1963, colour, Universal
Director: Stanley Donen; with Cary Grant,
Walter Matthau, and James Coburn

19. PARIS WHEN IT SIZZLES
USA 1964, colour, Paramount
Director: Richard Quine; with William Holden

20. MY FAIR LADY
USA 1964, colour / SuperPanavision, CBS/Warner
Director: George Cukor; with Rex Harrison

21. HOW TO STEAL A MILLION
USA 1966, colour / Panavision, 20th Century-
Fox / World Wide
Director: William Wyler; with Peter O'Toole

22. TWO FOR THE ROAD
England 1967, colour / Panavision, 20th Century-Fox
Director: Stanley Donen; with Albert Finney

23. WAIT UNTIL DARK
USA 1967, colour, Warner Seven Arts
Director: Terence Young; with Alan Arkin

24. ROBIN AND MARIAN
USA 1976, colour, Columbia / Rastar
Director: Richard Lester; with Sean Connery

25. BLOODLINE
USA 1979, colour, Paramount
Director: Terence Young; with Ben Gazzara,
James Mason

26. THEY ALL LAUGHED
USA 1981, colour, Time-Life / Moon Pictures
Director: Peter Bogdanovich; with Ben Gazzara

27. ALWAYS
USA 1989, colour, Amblin Entertainment
Director: Steven Spielberg; with Richard Dreyfuss

PICTURE CREDITS